AI for Learning

AI FOR EVERYTHING

Artificial intelligence (AI) is all around us. From driverless cars to game winning computers to fraud protection, AI is already involved in many aspects of life, and its impact will only continue to grow in future. Many of the world's most valuable companies are investing heavily in AI research and development, and not a day goes by without news of cutting-edge breakthroughs in AI and robotics.

The *AI for Everything* series will explore the role of AI in contemporary life, from cars and aircraft to medicine, education, fashion and beyond. Concise and accessible, each book is written by an expert in the field and will bring the study and reality of AI to a broad readership including interested professionals, students, researchers and lay readers.

AI for Immunology
Louis J. Catania

AI for Cars
Josep Aulinas & Hanky Sjafrie

AI for Digital Warfare
Niklas Hageback & Daniel Hedblom

AI for Art
Niklas Hageback & Daniel Hedblom

AI for Creativity
Niklas Hageback

AI for Death and Dying
Maggi Savin-Baden

AI for Radiology
Oge Marques

AI for Games
Ian Millington

AI for School Teachers
*Rose Luckin, Karine George &
Mutlu Cukurova*

AI for Learning
Carmel Kent & Benedict du Boulay

AI for Social Justice
Alan Dix and Clara Crivellaro

For more information about this series please visit:
https://www.routledge.com/AI-for-Everything/book-series/AIFE

AI for Learning

Carmel Kent

Benedict du Boulay

CRC Press
Taylor & Francis Group
Boca Raton London New York

CRC Press is an imprint of the
Taylor & Francis Group, an **informa** business

First Edition published 2022
by CRC Press
6000 Broken Sound Parkway NW, Suite 300, Boca Raton, FL 33487-2742

and by CRC Press
4 Park Square, Milton Park, Abingdon, Oxon, OX14 4RN

CRC Press is an imprint of Taylor & Francis Group, LLC

Library of Congress Cataloging-in-Publication Data

Names: Kent, Carmel, author. | Du Boulay, Ben, author.
Title: AI for learners / Carmel Kent, Benedict du Boulay.
Other titles: Artificial intelligence for learners
Description: First edition. | Boca Raton : CRC Press, 2022. |
Series: AI for everything | Includes bibliographical references and index.
Identifiers: LCCN 2021042773 | ISBN 9781032047553 (hardback) | ISBN 9781032039213 (paperback) | ISBN 9781003194545 (ebook)
Subjects: LCSH: Artificial intelligence--Educational applications.
Classification: LCC LB1028.43 .K46 2022 | DDC 371.33/4--dc23
LC record available at https://lccn.loc.gov/2021042773

ISBN: 978-1-032-04755-3 (hbk)
ISBN: 978-1-032-03921-3 (pbk)
ISBN: 978-1-003-19454-5 (ebk)

DOI: 10.1201/9781003194545

Typeset in Joanna
by Deanta Global Publishing Services, Chennai, India

CONTENTS

FOREWORD:
THE POWER OF LEARNING,
THE POWER OF AI

– **Rose Luckin**, Professor of Learner Centred Design
at the UCL Knowledge Lab in London

I remember the moment when I first came across the term 'artificial intelligence' or 'AI'. I was sitting on the sofa, pondering over the University of Sussex (Brighton, UK) course prospectus for undergraduate students. I had recently turned 30 but had not gone to university when I left school. I had gone straight into work, as was expected by my family. I'd worked in the financial services sector and had also taught in Further Education (FE) and secondary school. I had professional qualifications in finance and economics that I had achieved by day release from my full-time job, to study part time at the local FE college. But, as a mother of two young children, having taken a career break to be a 'stay-at-home' mum, I had now decided that perhaps it was a moment for a career change and a degree seemed like a great first step towards that new career.

I thought that I should apply to study for a degree in a similar territory to my professional qualifications, in order for my application to be successful. I had very few choices of universities that were in easy travelling distance from where I was living and enabled me to study while living at home. So I had settled on the University of Sussex as the most suitable institution for me. As I sat on the sofa, looking through the various course options available at Sussex, my mind wandered into thoughts about what being a student again would be like and the prospectus fell from my lap. When I picked it up again, the page it had rested on was describing a course in Computer Science and Artificial Intelligence.

This was the first time that I had come across the term 'artificial intelligence'. I read the course description. It was fascinating. Applicants did not need to have any prior experience with computers, and my existing A levels would be sufficient for admission to this course, provided I was fortunate enough to be selected from all the students who would be applying, of course.

I went out and bought one of the recommended textbooks, which was called **Gödel, Escher, Bach: An Eternal Golden Braid**, by Douglas Hofstadter. I read the textbook, it 'blew my mind' and I loved it. However, I confess, I certainly did not understand it all. The book had hooked me in, and I added the Computer Science and Artificial Intelligence degree course to my UCAS application form, along with all those that had a strong economics or finance theme. I was rejected from all the courses in economics but invited for an interview to study Computer Science and Artificial Intelligence. This was the start of a fascinating journey with AI and the way that it impacts teaching and learning.

From the moment I started my degree course, I absolutely adored it. I looked at everything through the lens of an educator, because that is what I had become. Not only had I taught face to face, but I had also enrolled as a tutor with the Rapid Results College: an early version of what might now be an online course provider, in order to add extra income to the family purse. I marked students' scripts, and I wrote course textbooks for the courses that I had once studied when working in finance. I therefore saw education as something that did not always have to be done on a face-to-face basis and I could see great possibilities for AI.

I had fully expected to be the oldest person on the course at Sussex. But, actually, I was not. There was another student who was older than me and a few who were a similar age. However, I was distinct in a way that I had not expected – I was one of only two female students taking the course. This dropped to me being the only female taking the course in the second year. This did not deter me, and I continued to enjoy my studies. I learned about things that I didn't even know existed as subjects. I would read the course description and shudder at the thought of trying to grasp the subject material. And, yet, as the different courses progressed, I enjoyed them more and more. I completed my degree successfully and continued to complete a PhD, also at the University of Sussex. My doctoral thesis involved building an AI system to help children aged 8–10 years learn about food chains and webs, no surprises there!

Why do I tell you this story about me? I tell you this story to illustrate that I was not a natural-born AI geek. I want you to know that it really is possible to get to grips with AI from a starting point of not knowing anything. I came to AI relatively late in life and struggled to understand the material and activities of my degree course. But the struggle was worth it, and I now want everyone to have the advantage that comes with understanding something about AI. This book talks about AI for Learning and is a great complement to a second volume, being published at the same time, called AI for Teachers. Therefore, whatever your perspective on education, there is an easy-to-understand book for you.

This book is written by experts who understand both AI and education and who care about learners and learning. Carmel Kent and Benedict du Boulay are people who can take you on a journey through which you will learn about the basics of AI with an extremely readable first chapter and about the different roles that AI can play and how AI systems have, do and will play these roles. AI can itself be a learner (Chapter 2), a tutor (Chapter 3) or a moderator

(Chapter 4). All the chapters explain the AI clearly and provide great examples to help you put your understanding in context. To conclude, you are invited to reflect on your learning and consider some of the challenging questions involved in designing responsible AI.

I believe that everyone should always be learning. So this is a book for everyone. Because all of us are learners. It's important that everyone understands what AI is, what it can do and what it cannot do. This is not the same as saying that everyone needs to learn how to program a deep neural network or understand the intricacies of a principal component analysis. It just means that everyone needs to understand the basics of the intelligence that it's possible to create under the umbrella of AI.

No matter what age you are, increasing your understanding of AI will help you navigate the increasingly technical world, more safely, and hopefully more enjoyably and successfully too. More and more jobs are and will be impacted by AI technologies. Most jobs are highly unlikely to be completely replaced by AI. But almost all of them are likely to be changed by AI. It is therefore essential to understand how to work alongside AI. And to do this, you need to understand the difference between artificial and human intelligence – to know the things that AI is better at than us humans, and to know the things that we are far better at than AI.

In this book, you will learn from the masters. I hope that you, like me, will find your life changed for the better by your increased understanding of AI.

INTRODUCTION: WHAT IS ALL THIS ABOUT AI IN EDUCATION?

Figure I.1 What is all this about AI in education? Illustrated by Yael Toiber Kent.

Synopsis: This chapter discusses this book's structure and who it is written for. We introduce the basic concepts around AI in education and the different ways that AI can be helpful (or unhelpful) to learners and teachers.

"Well done Bella, you have just learned something!", my Nix42 Virtual Assistant bot announces as it appears in front of me. "What? When? What did I just learn?" I'm confused, all I did was having my hot milk (which was too hot by the way). "I don't know, but according to your biometrics, you'll be ready to start schooling in four minutes" it replies. "So soon?!" It's 5:12PM, my older brother had finished school for the day just a few minutes ago, and it appears that my school day is just about to begin. Four minutes later, walking down the virtual corridor in my school, I pass by Kate walking with her Nix42 Premium. Kate used to be in my group just a couple of weeks ago, but for some reason she no longer complies with my group's similarity criteria. It might be that since her parents upgraded her virtual assistant, she no longer needs to share her data with the company producing our virtual assistants. Nevertheless, even when she was in my group I rarely spoke to her, since we have been using communication bots in class instead of talking to each other anyway. During the rest of my school day, Nix42 links me to an adaptive digital teacher, submits my essay to a plagiarism detection app, and gives me an instant score with feedback on the spot. My scores are then fed into our school's prediction engine, which refines my employability score at the end of each day. Today the probability of me getting my dream job as a fire fighter went down by 12% ... I am really confused. I am not sure what made my chances of getting my dream job reduced today, and I cannot even make any sense out of the feedback I received for my essay earlier. Since I am confused, I drop by Mrs Tunningham's office for a 'human touch' session, with the hope of finding some explanations. I know she most probably would not be able to offer an explanation, as she – like me, doesn't have the information behind the school's prediction engine. Still, I want at least to have someone human to talk to.

Inequality, unaccountability, confusion, lack of transparency, surveillance, mistrust, failed agency and isolation are some of the words which might come to mind when reading the above gloomy yet potentially realistic scenario about how learning might look while using artificial intelligence (AI) technologies. However, the reality could also look different. Very different. With this short book, we aim to equip people who practise, design, develop or simply care about education, with tools for critically evaluating AI systems used to support learning and teaching (Figure I.1).

Who are we? We are academics researching the field of artificial intelligence in education. In our long and fascinating experience working with many people who are passionate about developing and using educational technologies, we felt that the topic of artificial intelligence is frequently met with exaggerated hype or anxiety, more often with both. We felt that there is a need to explore this area and provide some evidence-based tools that would help practitioners to critically evaluate and design AI-based educational technologies.

This book is written in service to four key players in the EdTech ecosystem: education leaders, teachers, parents and EdTech developers, the first three of whom our students owe so much and the fourth stakeholder who has the power to create the tools to empower them. We had in mind an educational leader (such as a headteacher) who is looking to make an informed decision about using AI in their school. We imagined a teacher who might already have had this decision made for them but could benefit from critically evaluating and making an impact on the use of a specific AI technology in their particular class. We also considered parents trying to determine if and how their children will benefit from AI-based systems. Last, but not least, we imagined an EdTech designer or developer thinking about their business, seeking to use AI in a pedagogically sound and safe way. Clearly, you might find yourself belonging to more than one of these categories or none. In either case, we hope to feed your curiosity on the subject of AI in education.

Educational leaders, teachers, parents and EdTech developers do not necessarily share the same background, language and interests. At the same time, they all share a passion for education, and they all put the well-being of learners at the centre of their practice. A well-functioning education ecosystem cannot exist without those four key players sitting around the same table and engaging in a meaningful discussion. Educators and parents are those who understand the emotional, social, cultural and all-round circumstances of each and every single learner's journey. EdTech developers bring the expertise and access to the technological practice. Therefore, it is our hope in this book to equip them all with a shared evidence-based approach to tailor the right AI-based technology to their context.

There are several ways in which you can read this book. If you are generally curious about the role AI plays in our younger generations' lives, this book will help you explore the potential and the risks posed by AI from various angles of the learning experience. This includes how AI can be used as a learner, as a tutor, as well as a classroom moderator, in which case, you might prefer reading this book sequentially, chapter by chapter. Alternatively, if you are an EdTech designer or developer already thinking or working on an AI-based educational technology, or you are a teacher or parent already trying to critically evaluate or choose an AI-based educational technology, you might decide to dive directly into the chapter most relevant to the AI technology you have in mind.

In any case, we strongly advise you to start with this chapter as it provides a general introduction to the world of AI in education. Then, it would probably make sense to go through the first chapter, which will walk you through our five-step evaluation framework. The subsequent chapters then break down the learning experience into familiar components from the schooling ecosystem. Each such chapter will bring you some useful examples of how AI is (or could be) used in various parts of the educational ecosystem. Specifically, in Chapter 2 we discuss AI as a learner, in Chapter 3 AI as a tutor and in Chapter 4 AI as the classroom moderator.

At the end of each of these primary chapters we provide a clear example of how to apply the evaluation framework set out in Chapter 1 and demonstrate how the five-step framework could be applied to the relevant topic of each chapter. We hope that these examples will help you apply the five-step evaluation framework by yourself, in your own context (that is in your school, district, classroom or home). We conclude the book with an overall reflection and the distinction between what AI could do and what it should do, when it comes to education. Finally, to help you read this book, we have created a glossary at the end of the book. Concepts and terms defined in the glossary are underlined in the text to help you be reminded of them while reading.

BACKGROUND ON AI IN EDUCATION

AI has been overcomplicated over the years. Politically and economically, the mystification of AI has been a service to some sectors, while building an unjustifiable barrier for others. For those who are experts in human learning and teaching, who spend their days and nights thinking about the development of human beings' intelligence, we suggest looking at the topic of artificial intelligence from the point of view of its differences and commonalities to human intelligence and human learning. In that sense, AI simply refers to pieces of software or hardware (such as computer programs or robots) that might seem as if they are 'intelligent', that is acting or thinking humanly. Russel and Norvig [1] have suggested four categories of AI: first, AI that **thinks humanly**. This pertains to software or hardware pieces (we will refer to them as '**machines**' in general) that are involved in processes which are typically associated with human thinking, for example, AI for problem-solving and decision-making. The second category is **acting humanly**, which involves machines carrying out activities that humans would typically do, such as driving cars. The third category is machines **thinking rationally**, which differs from 'thinking humanly' in their focus on the computational processing of logics, rather than trying to mimic human thinking. For example, math exams automatic scoring, in which the logic behind assigning 'right' and 'wrong' rubrics is very straightforward. AlphaGo and its successor Muzero [2] are other good examples for AI systems 'thinking rationally' of 'good moves' in games such as Go and chess. The fourth category is machines **acting rationally**. Here, machines would take part in behaviours which are perceived to be 'intelligent' in human terms, such as chat bots.

AI <u>algorithms</u> developed in the past few decades can be roughly grouped into two main approaches. <u>The data-driven approach</u> (also called 'inductive reasoning') pertains to a machine collecting several data points or observations and generalising some logical conclusions

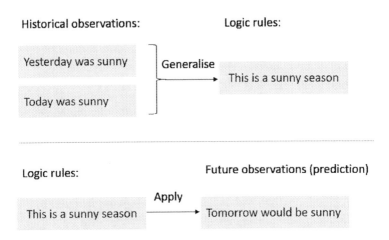

Figure I.2 Top – The data-driven approach: a logical rule is generalised based on a set of historical observations. Bottom – The logic-driven approach: a given logic rule is applied to future observations.

out of them. For example, consider the following 'algorithm': yesterday was a sunny day, today is a sunny day, which means that this is a sunny season. In contrast, the <u>logic-driven approach</u> (also called 'deductive reasoning') would begin with a given general logic rule and would then continue by applying this 'one source of truth' to the sample of points it observes. For example, consider the logic rule of 'this is the sunny season'. Applying it to future observations means that tomorrow would most probably be sunny. See a simplistic summary of the approaches in Figure I.2. Let us look at some examples.

THE LOGIC-DRIVEN APPROACH TO AI (ALSO TERMED 'DEDUCTIVE REASONING')

The 'logic-driven' approach to AI would typically entail applying a given general rule on a set of data points. For instance, based on the logical rule 'all rooms in a school are classrooms', an AI might notice a new room on the map of our school and conclude that it is most likely to be a classroom. One of the weaknesses of this approach is already apparent. Logical rules are generalisations, and generalisations are true until they aren't. To be more accurate, we would need to add many other, probably more refined rules (such as 'a classroom is a room with a whiteboard, residing inside a school') so that an AI can 'smartly' (and accurately) recognise classrooms by itself. Many of the first AI systems to appear, such as tutoring systems and other expert systems, were built on the logic-driven approach. For example, MYCIN was an early expert system that used AI to identify bacteria causing severe infections and to recommend the right antibiotics following medical guidelines [3].

The advantage of this approach is that the logic of the system can be clear and transparent. When a system's reasoning is transparent, the logic is relatively easy for us humans to agree with or refute. On the other hand, in reality, the number of rules required to formalise complex real world phenomena can very quickly increase exponentially. AI systems built on a too complex set of rules would typically result in a system that is very hard to maintain and prevent from making ambiguous or faulty reasoning.

THE DATA-DRIVEN APPROACH TO AI (ALSO TERMED 'INDUCTIVE REASONING')

When the logic-driven approach becomes too complex to implement, a data-driven approach would typically be considered. In this approach, we establish new logic rules based on many historical observations. For example, when examining our school's map, if an AI would recognise that the first ten rooms it encountered are classrooms, without an additional human supervision, the AI might conclude that 'all the rooms in the school are classrooms'. It is easy to see why this approach could fail. When there are simply not enough observations to derive a valid rule or when those observations are not sufficiently diverse or representative, the data-driven approach might easily induce nonsensible conclusions. For instance, it may have been merely by chance that the first ten rooms our AI system has encountered were classrooms, where in fact most of the rooms are not classrooms at all.

One of the most influential data-driven approaches to AI – and one of the most important subfields of AI overall – is called machine learning.

MACHINE LEARNING (ML):
A SUBFIELD OF DATA-DRIVEN AI

Machine learning is a subfield of artificial intelligence. It is the most widely used artificial intelligence method in the last 20 years, and it is based mostly on the data-driven approach. In that sense, ML models are developed on the basis of observed patterns that appear in the data.

The more observations or data points an ML model is able to take into account, the more accurate logic it would be able to generate. Tom Mitchell, one of the field's early contributors, referred to ML as 'improving automatically through experience'. This approach challenges the logic-driven approach and the notion of setting a logical 'source of truth' in advance, without even encountering any data observations. As the data changes, an ML algorithm would relearn it, picking up on the changing patterns to result in a slightly different logic.

Consider, for example, developing an AI solution that provides adaptive recommendations based on students' performance in a set of math problem-solving tasks. To come up with reasonable recommendations, we should predict the students' mastery level, based on their performance in the problem-solving tasks. Typically, if the AI system predicts that the student would do well in their final exam, the adaptive system would recommend an advanced module. However, if the AI system predicts they will not do well, it would recommend repeating more basic modules. How might we choose to predict if a student will do well in their final exam, based on their performance in the problem-solving tasks?

We might use a logic-driven approach and set in advance some rules, based on the logic of an expert math teacher. For example, the logic of the math teacher could be: "*a student is predicted to do well in* their final exam if they answer all ten quiz questions correctly on their first attempt in under 15 minutes".

As an alternative, an ML (data-driven) application would ignore the math teacher's (or any other) pre-set logic, but instead try to induce a new logical rule by examining all past records of students' performance on the problem-solving tasks, as well as their final exam grades. For example, the ML algorithm may determine that there is an "84% chance that a student would do well in their final exam if they were able to get eight out of ten quiz items right in less than three minutes, regardless of the last two items' results". Two different approaches then resulted in two different logics for predicting how well students will do in their final exam.

One crucial thing to notice is how sensitive an ML approach is to the specific set of students it has observed (or as we call it in ML lingo – the specific set of data points the ML algorithm 'was trained' on). The same ML system trained on a data resulted from a different age group would produce a different set of logic rules to predict success in the final exam. In that sense, the ML system is 'learning' from the patterns seen de facto in the data. An ML system (or any other data-driven AI for that matter) is a slave to the set of data points it is trained on. If the data set it is trained on is noisy, biased or not representative, the ML system would yield noisy (e.g. corrupted or distorted), biased and nonrepresentative results (or logic), no matter how smart its algorithm is.

To better understand how ML systems work, we would distinguish between two of the most commonly used families of ML algorithms: supervised ML and unsupervised ML.

TWO TYPES OF COMMONLY USED ML ALGORITHMS: SUPERVISED AND UNSUPERVISED LEARNING

The term 'supervised machine learning' refers to the process by which an ML algorithm is trained on a data set that was annotated (or as we call it in ML lingo – 'labelled') in advance by a human expert.

For example, having observed a huge number of pictures, which were labelled by humans as showing cats, Google is able to make a good guess about whether a newly observed image includes a cat [4].

In the example of the adaptive system used in the previous section, the historical students' final exam grades would be the 'labels' supervising the algorithm into what is a 'good' or a 'bad' outcome (high or low exam grades in this instance). These historical exam grades would 'supervise' the algorithm in picking up various data patterns in those historical records, which are typically associated with a 'good' or a 'bad' exam grade. An example of such a pattern which could be picked up from this data is that *"84% of the students who achieved a 'good' grade in their final exam were able to get eight out of ten quiz items right in less than three minutes, regardless of the last two items' results"*.

This process of identifying statistical patterns in the historical data set is what we call the **'training' of the algorithm**. After being trained, the algorithm would be able to advise or predict a final exam grade for a newly observed record of a student based on their performance in the math problem-solving task without having yet their final exam grade.

Two characteristics of supervised ML algorithms need to be taken into account. First of all, supervised ML algorithms are heavily dependent on the annotation (i.e., labelling) of a large volume of data. This might be a problem where the outcome needs to be judged by experts to whom access is limited. Secondly, supervised ML will be as biased as the labelling it is drawn from. If, for example, one school's mastery scoring system is more 'forgiving' than another's, the machine learning algorithm will accurately learn and preserve that bias.

Moreover, the reality is, we do not always have labelled (annotated) outcomes available to us. Either the data is not there, or we simply do not have access to a human expert who is able to label a large number of students' records for us.

Alternatively, we might have the labelled outcome but prefer to not use it. For example, we might have the students' records for the math problem-solving tasks, but we are not interested in predicting their final exam grades. Instead, we might wish to learn other patterns hidden in the data. For example, we might want to identify groups of students exhibiting similar patterns of problem-solving in order to tutor the groups separately or to use different methods of intervention. In this case, we are not looking to be supervised by any labelled outcome. Instead, this type of ML algorithms is called **unsupervised learning.**

To read more on the history of AI, the interested reader is referred to [5], [6] and [7]. To learn about ML, the interested reader is referred to [8].

THE OPPORTUNITIES OF AI IN EDUCATION

AIED (AI in Education) has been a research field for over 45 years. It brings together AI and the research discipline of the learning sciences. While AI is focused on the intersection of computational methods mimicking or complementing human intelligence, the <u>learning sciences</u> are focused on understanding the processes around effective or ineffective human learning and its implications on the design and implementation of learning tools and instructional methods.

Many AIED systems are considered as a mix of three models (or components), see Figure I.3, namely, the pedagogical model, the domain model and the learner model. In designing the pedagogical

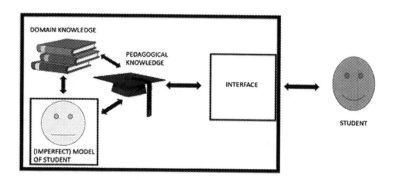

Figure I.3 Conceptual architecture of an AIED system.

model, the systems' designers would need to consider how to properly express teaching methods (such as how to deliver effective feedback and how to use worked examples). In the domain model, the taught subject knowledge would need to be modelled (for example, what are the main concepts and skills associated with these concepts). The learner model embodies the changing cognitive, affective and behavioural attributes of the learner. In other words, these models are descriptions of what is to be taught (the domain model), how to teach it (the pedagogical model), and how far the student has understood it and is able to apply the skills associated with it (the learner model).

A simplified architecture of an AIED system consists of the three models mentioned above, together with an interface through which the system and the learners communicate. We develop this simplified architecture in Chapter 2 where we introduce some specific AIED systems.

As teachers and AIED researchers, we strongly believe that AI **can and should be used** in everyday learning and teaching scenes, both in the classroom and outside of it (see [9] and [10]). It has a huge potential to ease the burden on schools and teachers, to make learning more effective, inclusive, streamlined and engaging, to make assessment relevant and pedagogically driven and to help students prepare for life as adults. In this book, we will bring many examples of those opportunities of AI in education. To read more background on AI in education – please see [11].

The wordle in Figure I.4 illustrates many examples in which AI is used in education.

THE RISKS OF AI IN EDUCATION

Facial recognition in schools [12], racists bots [13], discriminatory algorithms [14,15], biased grading [16], algorithmic bias [17], the aspiration to replace human teachers [18] and many more horror stories associated with the use of AI in education [19] constantly cloud the sky of EdTech and often overshadow the many opportunities

Figure I.4 Examples of the applications of AIED.

that AI can offer. The increasing use of AI imposes another set of challenges on top of the risks inherent to the general use of EdTech, such as: bias and discrimination; the potential denial of autonomy and rights; invasions of privacy; flawed, unsafe or poor-quality results; and, finally, bad PR (see Figure I.5).

While AI tools and techniques have been in development since the 1950s, with their applications to education starting in the 1970s, concerns about their impact on society pre-date even that (see for example the film **The Golem** (1915) and earlier stories about statues being brought to life [20]). The use of AI in mainstream software systems, however, has enabled a considerable advance in the ethical debate around AI in recent years, and some practical tools and plans have been devised in order to avoid the problems outlined above.

Figure I.5 Examples of risks associated with using AIED.

AI in education is a particularly sensitive area (see [21] and [22]) and requires a step-by-step inspection of the product development process in order to make sure it is being designed, developed and utilized in a sensible, safe and productive way.

Floridi and Cowls [23] have developed a useful ethical framework, based on four 'traditional' bioethics principles (namely, Benficience, Non-Maleficience, Autonomy and Justice), and with a fifth added principle to encompass another area not targeted by the existing four – Explicability. Floridi and Cowls' framework, while not specifically designed for education, has proved to be a very useful tool for evaluating and designing AI systems in education. The following is a brief description of the five elements that should be audited carefully to ensure safe development of an artificial intelligence application:

1. **Beneficence (doing good)**: promoting well-being, preserving dignity and sustaining the planet, *"prioritise human well-being as an outcome in all system designs"*, *"ensure that AI technologies benefit and empower as many people as possible"*;

2. **Non-maleficence (not doing harm)**: privacy, security and 'capability caution' cautions against various negative consequences of overusing or misusing AI technologies;

3. **Autonomy**: the power to decide, striking a balance between the decision-making power we retain for ourselves and that which we delegate to artificial agents *"must not impair [the] freedom of human beings to set their own standards and norms"*;

4. **Justice**: preserving solidarity, avoiding unfairness, relating to the use of AI to correct past wrongs such as eliminating unfair discrimination, promoting diversity and preventing the rise of new threats to justice;

5. **Explicability**: enabling the other principles through intelligibility, transparency and accountability. *"The situation is inherently unequal: a small fraction of humanity is currently engaged in the development of a set of technologies that are already transforming the everyday lives of almost everyone else"*.

We warmly suggest using this framework of five principles to critically evaluate various AI applications in educational contexts, which we also do throughout the book. Specifically, the more recently added principle of explicability has significant importance in educational artificial intelligence evaluation. It consists of two very important and highly connected subprinciples: explainability and accountability. If a decision or recommendation is made by, aided by or based on an AI system and it cannot be easily communicated and explained to people using human logic and language, it might be extremely difficult to assess its accuracy. As a result, it would be very difficult for human beings to establish trust following decisions made by AI. In the AI research field, considerable effort is focused on interpreting and explaining the predictions and recommendations of complex AI models, which when not transparent and explainable are called 'black box' systems [24].

The accountability of the decision-maker is also a necessary element of trust, whether it is an AI system or a human operating it. Accountability requires discussions about responsibility, deliberation and moral values, none of which can be addressed by machines. Therefore, when discussing accountability, it emphasises how asymmetrical the division of labour is between the human beings responsible for the development of an AI system and those affected by that system. Accountability is a must in life-changing decisions, such as in education. Also, the well-communicated existence of an accountable person or group most often diffuses backward and can make the design, development, testing and deployment processes of the systems to be carefully carried out (see some approaches and strategies that have been discussed to address accountability in AI systems [25]).

If there is one message to be taken away from this book, it would be that AI should not be used just for the sake of using AI. There should be a well-thought out reason for complementing human intelligence; the risks that come with using it should be deeply deliberated throughout the whole process of designing and deploying AI-based educational applications. Most of all, learners and teachers must be kept as centrally active stakeholders steering this discussion. If anything, our hope is that after reading the coming chapters, AI would not be seen as a utopian (or dystopian) mystified creature but as a down-to-earth utility held confidentially in human hands, as it should be.

REFERENCES

1. Russel, S., & Norvig, P. (2016). *Artificial Intelligence: A modern approach*. Malaysia: Pearson Education Limited. doi:10.1017/S0269888900007724

2. Schrittwieser, J., Antonoglou, I., Hubert, T., Simonyan, K., Sifre, L., Schmitt, S., Guez, A., Lockhart, E., Hassabis, D., Graepel, T., Lillicrap, T., and Silver, D (2020, December 20). MuZero: Mastering Go, chess, shogi and Atari without rules. https://deepmind.com/blog/article/muzero-mastering-go-chess-shogi-and-atari-without-rules

3. Buchanan, B. G., & Shortliffe, E. H. (1984). Rule-based expert systems: the MYCIN experiments of the Stanford Heuristic Programming Project.

4. Google Cloud, Vision AI. https://cloud.google.com/vision

5. Kilani, A., Hamida, A. B., & Hamam, H. (2018). Artificial Intelligence review. In *Encyclopedia of information science and technology*. M. Khosrow-Pour, Ed. (4th ed., pp. 106–119). IGI Global. Hershey, PA, USA.

6. Gonsalves, T. (2019). The summers and winters of Artificial Intelligence. In *Advanced methodologies and technologies in artificial intelligence, computer simulation, and human-computer interaction* (pp. 168–179). IGI Global.

7. Menzies, T. (2003). 21st-century AI: Proud, not smug. *IEEE Intelligent Systems*, 18(3), 18–24.

8. Shalev-Shwartz, S., & Ben-David, S. (2014). *Understanding machine learning: From theory to algorithms*. Cambridge University Press, New York, NY, USA, 2014. ISBN 1107057132, 9781107057135.

9. du Boulay, B. (2016). Artificial Intelligence as an effective classroom assistant. *IEEE Intelligent Systems*, 31(6), 76–81.

10. du Boulay, B. (2019). Escape from the Skinner Box: The case for contemporary intelligent learning environments. *British Journal of Educational Technology*, 50(6), 2902–2919.

11. Kent, C. (2019). Evidence summary: Artificial Intelligence in education. Retrieved from https://eetn.eu/dam/jcr:a29ff41e-2900-4468-8a60-66a4104dd46a/EDUCATE_AIeducation.pdf

12. Herold, B. (2018, July 18). Facial-Recognition Systems Pitched as School-Safety Solutions, Raising Alarms. EducationWeek. https://www.edweek.org/leadership/facial-recognition-systems-pitched-as-school-safety-solutions-raising-alarms/2018/07;

13. Vincent, J. (2016, March 24). Twitter taught Microsoft's AI chatbot to be a racist asshole in less than a day. The Verge. https://www.theverge.com/2016/3/24/11297050/tay-microsoft-chatbot-racist

14. Kent, C. & Lepkowska, D. (2020, August 13). A national lesson in data modelling and analytics. Medium. https://medium.com/educate-ventures/a-national-lesson-in-data-modelling-and-analytics-c3007e896d45

15. Barbaschow, A. (2017, July 12). Should big data be used to discourage poor students from university? ZDNet. https://www.zdnet.com/article/should-big-data-be-used-to-discourage-poor-students-from-university

16. MacMillan, D. & Anderson, N. (2019, October 14). Student tracking, secret scores: How college admissions offices rank prospects before they apply. The

Washington Post. https://www.washingtonpost.com/business/2019/10/14/colleges-quietly-rank-prospective-students-based-their-personal-data/

17. Feathers, T. (2019, August 20). Flawed Algorithms Are Grading Millions of Students' Essays. VICE. https://www.vice.com/en/article/pa7dj9/flawed-algorithms-are-grading-millions-of-students-essays

18. Hanbury, M. (2019, May 17). Elon Musk awards $10 million prize to 2 startups replacing teachers with tech. INSIDER. https://www.businessinsider.com/elon-musk-awards-10-million-prize-to-kids-learning-startups-2019-5?r=US&IR=T

19. Watters, A. (2019, December 31). The 100 Worst Ed-Tech Debacles of the Decade. Haceducation. http://hackeducation.com/2019/12/31/what-a-shitshow

20. Samuel, A. L. (1960). Some moral and technical consequences of automation – a refutation. *Science*, 132(3429), 741–742.

21. The Institute for Ethical AI in Education. (2020). The ethical framework for AI in education. Retrieved from https://fb77c667c4d6e21c1e06.b-cdn.net/wp-content/uploads/2021/03/The-Institute-for-Ethical-AI-in-Education-The-Ethical-Framework-for-AI-in-Education.pdf

22. Williamson, B. (2018). Silicon startup schools: Technocracy, algorithmic imaginaries and venture philanthropy in corporate education reform. *Critical Studies in Education*, 59(2), 218–236.

23. Floridi, L., Cowls, J., Beltrametti, M., Chatila, R., Chazerand, P., Dignum, V., ... & Schafer, B. (2018). AI4People – An ethical framework for a good AI society: Opportunities, risks, principles, and recommendations. *Minds and Machines*, 28(4), 689–707.

24. Lacave, C., & Díez, F. J. (2002). A review of explanation methods for Bayesian networks. *The Knowledge Engineering Review*, 17(2), 107–127.

25. Baker, R. S., & Hawn, A. (2021, March 1). Algorithmic bias in education. EdArXiv preprint. doi:10.35542/osf.io/pbmvz

1

HOW DO I TELL THE DIFFERENCE BETWEEN GOOD AI AND BAD?

OR - ABOUT OUR FIVE-STEP EVALUATION OF CAKE MIXES

Figure 1.1 How do I tell the difference between good AI and bad? Illustrated by Yael Toiber Kent.

Synopsis: This chapter describes a simple five-step process for evaluating AI-based technologies for education. If you are a parent or an educator, following these five steps should assist you in evaluating the use of a new AI-based technology in your classroom or in learning at home. It will help you cut through the sales talk to see which

DOI: 10.1201/9781003194545-1

AI systems are useful for you, which have the potential to harm and which are simply not suitable. If you are an EdTech developer or designer and you have an idea about how to use AI in learning or teaching, following these five steps will help you in making design choices aiming at developing an AI-based technology with a real educational value. This way, your product would not join the shelf of AI-based white elephants that no learner, teacher or parent would actually use effectively.

Think about the framework as evaluating the quality of a marriage or a partnership: a partnership between humans and machines. This partnership would look completely different in different educational settings or contexts. As always with education – everything is in the context, right? For example, evaluating the use of an AI system to tutor preschool children's reading would look completely different (and would take completely different considerations into account) than evaluating an AI system that trains teachers. The outline of the five steps is the same, but it is totally up to you to apply your own context on top of it.

This chapter will walk you through these five steps, and the rest of the chapters will provide you examples of how to apply the five step process in specific educational contexts, so that you can go on and 'write your own chapter', fill it with the details about the learners, the domain knowledge and the pedagogy you know best – and evaluate how AI should – or should not – be used (Figure 1.1).

Our evaluation process (summarised in Figure 1.2) consists of four main steps, while the fifth is about going back and iterating through the whole process when needed. In the first step, we consider what each partner does best. In other words, we would try to map what we (human beings) are good at and what AI systems are good at, in the context of each specific educational challenge. Having this distinction in mind, in the second step we examine how this partnership looks (or rather should look) like. We choose the way in which human intelligence and artificial intelligence might work together, again – to achieve the specific educational challenge in mind. When the collaboration architecture is in place, the third step is to list the ways in which this partnership might

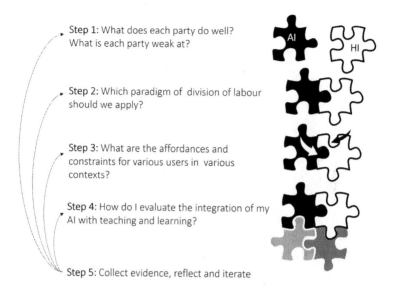

Step 1: What does each party do well? What is each party weak at?

Step 2: Which paradigm of division of labour should we apply?

Step 3: What are the affordances and constraints for various users in various contexts?

Step 4: How do I evaluate the integration of my AI with teaching and learning?

Step 5: Collect evidence, reflect and iterate

Figure 1.2 Five iterative steps in assessing AI in learning and teaching.

open opportunities or constraints to the learning process we have in mind. The fourth step is to specify how to use our evaluated AI technology as a learning or teaching activity. Lastly, the fifth step focuses on reflecting on how well the technology works within the chosen learning context, which aspects need to be rethought and how to redesign and evaluate again a newer, better, evidence-based version.

ON WHEELS, CAKE MIXES AND CLIPPY

A century ago, flour companies invented cake mixes. American housewives were promised that they would get a desirable product at an affordable price, as well as being freed them from laborious hours in the kitchen. They were tempted by the dream of using their time more efficiently, instead of 'wasting' it on searching for a recipe (remember, Google was not there all along!), bothering to find the individual fresh ingredients, measuring, mixing and worrying about countless matters that could go wrong in the process. With the new cake mixes – even nonexpert bakers could achieve an expert result! Could anyone with their right mind refuse such an offer? **Yes**, as it turns out. How surprised the cake-mix manufacturers were to realise that their target audience – housewives – still preferred to search, mix, clean and stand for hours on their tired feet. Why would they? What went wrong?

Ernest Dichter, a psychologist and a marketing consultant hired to solve the mystery, used focus groups to transform a whole industry in the 50s, with one simple magic ingredient: a fresh egg.

In fact, the magic ingredient was not the egg itself but rather the **exclusion** of the egg powder from the cake mix and its reinstatement into the hands of the home baker as a fresh egg. This way, home baking would not feel 'fully automated'. In other words, Dichter had restored the <u>human-in-the-loop</u>. Years later, this transformational pivot is still being taught in marketing classes as the perfect example of how irrational we humans are. The problem with the cake mix, marketing students are being taught, is that home bakers didn't feel emotionally invested enough by just adding water [1]. Baking had been presented as 'an emotional activity', and the 'repositioning' of the egg had been presented as a foxy deception, which made the 'irrational' bakers regain their emotional investment and feeling of control.

But were those home bakers really irrational? And how did a baking story find its way into an education book on AI? Well, for one thing – baking, much like educating, is a science and an art. Following a good recipe and using a mix of ingredients is a must in both professions. However, the 'glue' cannot be synthesised, whether it is an egg or personal human feedback. A factory-made batch of identical cakes might not be exactly right every day for every person. It takes an experienced and perceptive baker to finesse the final touch, take into account the room temperature and consider the various preferences and potential allergies of the cake's potential eaters.

Every amateur baker knows that baking is an act of love, cherishing and intent. Just because something can be taken out of human hands, it does not mean it should.

Cake mixes, the wheel, the printing press, the computer and even technologies which are almost taken for granted today, such as the personal calculator, were designed to augment human abilities and achieve our goals by complementing human deficiencies (such as memory decay or distortion) with technology's **unfair advantage**. Technology's unfair advantage is the capacity that it undoubtedly and uniquely has over us humans (such as the ability to store a large amount of data and process it quickly).

Evidently, when the cake mix was taken completely out of the human's hands, things did not go well. Similarly, Microsoft's Word designers in the 1990s assumed that people would interact with an automatic assistant. As it turns out, the designed digital assistant (called Clippy for those of us too young to have met it) did not adhere to many of the social norms expected by people from 'an assistant', such as getting to know the person it was trying to help [2]. Eventually Clippy, which was introduced in 1995, did not endure beyond the early 2000s' upgrade of Office.

So how do we – educators, parents and EdTech designers – ensure that a technology effectively supports the needs of learners, as well as ourselves, without penalising our or their sense of being able, sense of trust, and our fundamental right to develop our own human qualities and excel in what we are good at? How do we make this human–machine partnership work properly?

In this book, we suggest that a robust design of a human–machine partnership can be achieved only when we (educational experts or designers) gain a profound understanding of what are our (human) unfair advantages and what are the augmenting technology's unfair advantages. These unfair advantages should be sensitively considered in the context of a particular task or need (whether it is being able to bake a cake happily or in an educational context, as we will examine in this book). Unlike a typical human–human collaboration, in a human–machine collaboration, we are dealing with two parties who are very far apart in terms of their skill sets. It is only when we have figured out what each party is best at, and where they fall short, can we get on to design AI-based systems.

In the rest of this chapter, we will detail the five steps of our framework to design and evaluate AI systems in education.

STEP 1: MAP OUT OUR/THEIR UNFAIR ADVANTAGES

AI systems are good at picking out patterns from large datasets and reapplying them (potentially repeatedly and fast) onto similar datasets. For example, a <u>machine learning (ML)</u> model trained on historical data of a specific population, predicting the efficacy of a specific drug, is likely to predict the efficacy of this drug accurately on a new population, that is – given that this is the same drug and that the new population is very similar to the one it was trained on.

Furthermore, algorithms, and in particular AI algorithms, are heavily reliant on hardware. Advancements in storage capabilities, computing and parallelism have enabled AI to increase its performance and ultimately its popularity over recent years. The 'memory device' called the Internet and the immense acceleration in computing power have armed AI applications with an unfair advantage over humans in terms of speed and memory capacity.

One of humans' unfair advantages is our ability to comprehend worlds, scenes or situations we might not have seen before and that are not rigidly predictable, well defined and certain; AI falls short in this ability. AI is at its finest when recalling, searching and recognising **well-described, narrow worlds**. Playing Go or Chess, image classification, speech recognition, handwriting transcription, digital assistants (such as Siri and Alexa) and even autonomous driving – to some extent – are all challenges that are often well defined, narrow and relatively static in their scope of logic. These are challenges that often requires the ability to quickly and accurately process large datasets. These are all examples of AI's unfair advantage over us. Even as knowledgeable, trained and seasoned humans, we will always possess a limited short-term memory that falls short when attempting to do as well as machines in these kinds of task.

Human beings are born with a limited memory and cognitive processing ability. We typically compensate for this shortage with far-from-ideal mental shortcuts, such as heuristics, schemas and scripts. For example, we might use rules of thumb, educated guesses and stereotypes to get us through everyday decisions such as whether to cross the road, how to approach a person we do not know or when to take the bus in order to get to our meeting on time. Obviously, in addition to allowing us to make effective and quick decisions [3], such mental shortcuts can also lead us to make mistakes and introduce biases in our decision-making (such as confirmation bias, anchoring bias, group-favouritism, limited attention span and the framing effect).

AI systems, despite having their own blind spots, don't need to employ such shortcuts, as their processing capacity is far less limited. Consequently, AI algorithms are well-positioned to assist us in identifying our own human biases and making better-informed decisions.

Humanity's unfair advantage consists of our ability to transfer skills between different domains, to imagine, to adapt, to connect disparate worlds and to pull new meanings out of these connections. AI systems are still limited in their ability to assign sensible semantics to new data and patterns, to doubt and to challenge them. For example, an algorithm would struggle to figure out if an image includes a kitten or a scoop of ice cream with two raisins, as long as they are composed of a similar set of coloured pixels. This is an example of humans' unfair advantage in identifying objects, which stems from human use of semantic schemas.

A human observer finds it very easy to identify which images show a kitten and in which ice cream appears. On the contrary, an AI algorithm can only see an array of coloured pixels, which in the kittens and ice cream scoop with raising – might look very similar.

Moreover, AI is certainly limited in its ability to transfer data patterns it learned from one context to another. In the previous example about an AI system predicting the efficacy of a drug, the efficacy data was inferred from a prediction algorithm, trained on a specific population. Trying to predict the drug efficacy on a new population might yield disastrous results.

"The quest for 'artificial flight' succeeded when the Wright brothers and others stopped imitating birds and started using wind tunnels and learning about aerodynamics," Russel and Norvig write in their book [4]. The sweet spot in AI system design is the moment at which AI systems stop mimicking humans and take advantage of how different the unfair advantages of humans and AI are.

Luckin [5] identified the elements of human intelligence that do not have a genuine equivalent in 'artificial cognition'. These elements include social intelligence (which typically guides humans in social interactions), meta-cognitive intelligence (the ability to interpret our own mental state) and perceived self-efficacy (our judgement about our own capability, knowledge, emotions and motivations). Luckin's list is characterized by humans' ability to identify the extent to which they know and feel themselves. Additionally, the list also points to humans' ability to recognise other human beings as similar creatures to themselves while reflecting on what they know and feel.

STEP 2: HOW CAN WE THINK OF HUMAN–AI COLLABORATION?

When we understand in what way humans and machines can complement each other's strengths and weaknesses, we are better positioned to take the next step and design how to bring them together to meet our specific educational challenge. Looking at the main paradigms for the division of labour between humans and AI systems (Figure 1.3 below), it is worthwhile looking back at when the concept of AI first came about. John McCarthy, one of the pioneers of the AI field, defined AI in 1956, as "*the science and engineering of making intelligent machines that have the ability to achieve goals like humans do*". This definition was very typical of the earliest paradigm of the human–AI division of labour, where AI systems were thought of as (or were hoped to become) 'thinking machines'. Some examples of this paradigm were ELIZA, the text-based Rogerian therapist [6], PARRY, a schizophrenic simulator [7], and many 'expert systems' developed in the 1980s and the 1990s. With the progression of the field, new paradigms evolved.

In Figure 1.3, we present five paradigms of human and machine interaction and suggest some perspectives to assess AI systems.

The uppermost paradigm in the illustration, termed 'thinking machines' and probably the earliest to gain traction, was focused on

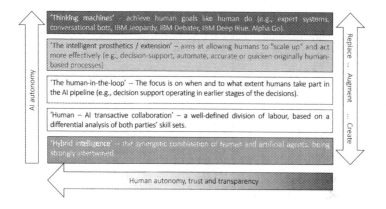

Figure 1.3 Human–AI division of labour paradigms. The arrow on the left illustrates how AI autonomy increases as we move up the ladder of collaboration paradigms. The double-sided arrow on the right shows that the paradigms are based on the idea of replacing the human as we move up the ladder and on creating something new as we go down. The middle is rather focused on augmenting humans. The bottom arrow reads into the colour scheme. The lighter the colour, the more emphasis is placed on human autonomy, trust and transparency.

AI duplicating and replacing human capabilities. Going downwards in the illustration above, 'the intelligent extension' and 'the human in the loop' shifted the focus to human augmentation, rather than replacement and automation. These shifts were mostly attributed to some serious faults and inadequacies of the 'thinking machines' paradigm coming to light. As in the cake-mix story, this pushback arose from the realisation that leaving humans out of the loop is simply too risky.

All of the five paradigms are based on a computational understanding and modelling of human behaviour. Some of these paradigms rely on the assumption that we (humankind) have figured out human behaviour and that we are ready to model or computerise it. This assumption is still very far from reality, at least at the time in which these sentences are being written. We believe that it is progress in the understanding of human behaviour and cognition, rather than in automation, that will most likely lead to the next major breakthrough in the field of AI.

Each of the five paradigms in Figure 1.3 represents a range of approaches instead of representing a single unified realm. The difference between these paradigms more often lies in where their focus is rather than anywhere else. For example, the 'human in the loop' paradigm, which came out as a pushback to the two upper paradigms, is focused on identifying to what extent and when in the AI development and operational process, human actors take a role other than mere users. When looking at some of the newest technological advancements in AI (such as the automation of ML modelling frameworks, e.g. the feature engineering process that deep learning approaches have automated), the 'human in the loop' approach would focus on identifying the parts in the AI development process that are still left in human hands. Those parts could be, for example, a human expert labelling the outcomes as 'good' or 'bad' in a supervised ML algorithm, or a human making the final decision after being supported by an AI system. Regardless of how and when the human is participating, the human-in-the-loop paradigm assumes an AI dominance in the process, and its focus is on where and how a human actor comes in.

Think for example of driverless cars. These are designed as an autonomous technology, but still require humans putting their hands near the steering wheel ready to take over at a moment's notice when the autonomous car is evidently about to make a seriously wrong decision. To position humans in this straitjacket of constant vigilance for any sudden shortcoming in the machine's behaviour is to completely misunderstand what humans are good at and what they are bad at. Think of the enormous time it took people to trust lifts and to use them without a human operator, although they were already fully automated.

The shift to the two bottom paradigms in Figure 1.3 expresses the movement of the focus away from machine dominance to partnership models. As such, both the two bottom partnership paradigms require a profound understanding of joint actions in teams (composed of humans and machines). Both those paradigms are focused on how we can utilise the skill sets of both humans and machines to achieve better outcomes than when carrying the same task dominated by either humans or machines. Other than that, these two paradigms significantly differ from each other in their collaboration architecture and their underlying assumptions.

To better understand the distinction between the human–AI transactive collaboration paradigm and the hybrid intelligence paradigm, let us briefly discuss the architectures of collaboration. In her book, Salmons [8] discusses six types of collaboration: reflection, dialogue, constructive review, parallel collaboration, sequential collaboration and synergistic collaboration (see in Figure 1.4).

In both Salmons's parallel and sequential collaboration types, different members of the group (machines and humans in our context) work on their individual components, which would be integrated eventually to a combined (human–AI) product. However, in a synergistic collaboration, the melding of individual contributions (of machines and humans) is less well defined, and so they are strongly intertwined, to a point where the user of such a system would not necessarily be able to identify who did what. As Salmons points out, synergistic collaboration requires a higher level of trust between the collaborating parties and of the user, because of these blurred boundaries.

Research in the field of collaboration models typically examines how different the capabilities of the various parties are and how that difference affects the performance of the team and its collective product. One very interesting theoretical approach derived from this line of research is the "transactive memory" theory [9]. This theory grows out of Wegner's observations of married couples who developed a division of labour, which is based on a well-defined understanding of what each partner is good at. Using this model, it was found that groups showing behavioural indicators of transactive memory performed better at group tasks than groups in which the division of labour was not based on the notion of unfair advantages [10].

Similar to the married couples in Wegner's study, the 'human–AI transactive collaboration' paradigm (second from the bottom in

Taxonomy of Collaboration

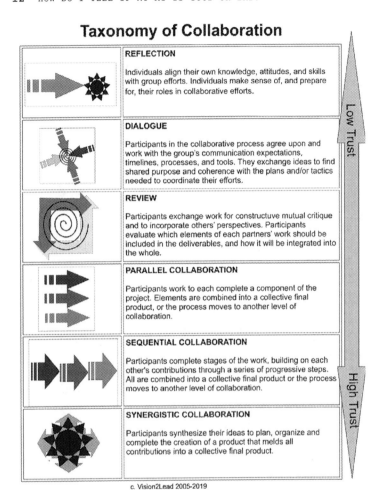

c. Vision2Lead 2005-2019

Figure 1.4 Taxonomy of collaboration (Salmons, 2019).

Figure 1.3) is based on the assumption that humans and machines are **very different** in their skill sets. Consequently, the architecture of AI systems in this paradigm is based on a well-defined mapping of those differences, such as the one carried out in Step 1.

Unlike the 'hybrid intelligence' paradigm, which is focused on a synergy between humans and machines, the 'human–AI transactive collaboration' paradigm does not assume that artificial actors are simply yet another actor but requires a **specialised and proactive assignment of tasks** that utilises their differences in competence. An example of an AI system operating under the 'human–AI transactive collaboration' paradigm might be one which assists in reducing common human biases such as a bias towards short-term rewards or confirmation bias [11].

Substantial work in the field of artificial multi-actors (also called multi-agent systems) has been focused on distributing tasks and monitoring plan progression. Yet human actors' collaboration works very differently (and therefore needs to be modeled differently) compared to artificial actors. This is due to a mix of social factors such as cooperation and internal and external motivation.

Real-world environments are rarely static. Both internal (such as internal motivation) and external factors (such as people's availability) affect their team composition, preferences and interpersonal interactions. Since, in the real world, factors change all the time, it is very hard to manage 'hybrid intelligence' systems, where there is no clear division of labour between its parties. This is why hybrid intelligence systems are strongly reliant on their ability to quickly and safely adapt to changes. While there have been advances in the field of ML in recent years, this on-the-fly adaptability is still technically challenging in complex contexts. It puts a huge burden on the development of hybrid intelligence systems, as well as on their accountable deployment. Not only can safety and reliability potentially be compromised, but also a full synergistic collaboration of human and AI actors often leads to situations in which information relating to decisions is unclear, and the right to dispute a decision is not possible [12]. This is because it is unclear who does what and who is responsible for which task. For example, consider the following 'hybrid intelligence' use case, taken from Akata et al. [13]:

> *A child with learning difficulties is supported by a team in which the child's remedial teacher, an educational therapist, and a Nao robot collaborate. Together, they design a targeted learning program, monitor progress, and provide encouragement.*

> *The robot combines expertise from the human team members with its own observations and gives advice on possible adjustments to the program. Interacting with the Nao robot helps the child to stay focused and have fun for a longer period of time.*

In this case, the Nao robot's skills are used throughout the interaction. It is operating as a team member, team moderator and advisor and also interacts with the child directly. This architecture places high demands on the robot's ability to explain its judgements and the ability to adapt in real time to any change in the child's behaviour, the human team members' behaviour and any changes in the external environment (such as those which were forced by COVID-19, for example). In other words, the intertwining of the robot's and human actor's tasks exposes the system to risks. Hybrid intelligence may actually hold some of the assumptions used by the 'thinking machine' paradigm when placing an artificial agent in the midst of a very complex human situation. As such, this intertwined architecture requires high levels of trust from the humans working with it or alternatively, if the trust cannot be established, some sort of regulation.

Having said that, based on a 'distributed cognition' [14] point of view, in which human and machine actors are part of a shared 'cognitive system', the hybrid intelligence paradigm is probably a very good choice when considering complex problem-solving systems. Rather than 'fencing' in human skills to well-defined components and points in time during the process of creating ML models, complex problem-solving applications might require a continuous and strong coupling of humans and AI actors [15], which the hybrid intelligence collaboration paradigm is ideal for.

To summarise, when choosing between the five human–AI division of labour paradigms in Figure 1.3, we suggest asking ourselves a number of questions. For instance:

- When considering use cases such as the cake mix, Clippy or the supportive Nao robot, what level of trust do we expect human users to have in the system?
- To what extent could the AI system (or its designer) be made accountable or responsible for any consequences in my system?

- What level and type of coordination between various (human and AI) actors would be required [16] by our chosen paradigm? Would the effort of putting this level of coordination in place be worth the system's merits?
- What is the difference between the various (human and AI) actors' skills and cognition as mapped in Step 1, and to what extent should this distinction be transparent to the system's users?
- To what extent do we expect the AI system to be perceived as human (like in the case of Clippy or the Nao robot)? Can my AI actor be attributed with moral roles or capacities? To what extent do my AI actors require an understanding of the human actors (or of the human behaviour in general)? For example, will the AI actor need to comprehend the world of ethics? And if it does, how can it acquire this ethical line of thought? Does it need to understand reciprocity, kinship, social norms, meta-cognition or culture [17]? Attributing human values to AI actors typically causes human users to expect explanations for some decisions. Moreover, they would expect those explanations to be given in the same way humans are used to explain their decisions (i.e. everyday explanations). Once this expectation is not realised, trust is highly jeopardised [18].
- How exposed are humans' personal data to various (external and internal) parties?
- What scrutiny processes are in place for our AI systems? For example, to make sure the system is not discriminating unfairly?

STEP 3: AN EVALUATION OF THE AI LEARNING AFFORDANCES

After mapping the unfair advantages and risks associated with human vs. machine actors, in this section we take the next step and consider how the AI system would be used by people.

To do this, we use the term 'technological affordance'. Technological affordance in our context refers to both the "*perceived and actual properties of a technology, which determine just how it could be used*" [19]. For example, an email application can have different affordances for different users. It can afford us the ability to communicate asynchronously with our loved ones, a way to manage our professional network, and as storage of exchanges. However, email does not afford synchronous communication in the way that a phone call does; nor does it afford us using body language to communicate [20].

Affordances are not necessarily based on technological features or abilities, and they are not always aligned with what the technology designers meant to be affording. It is a much more subjective and dynamic concept, which refers to the capabilities (and limitations) a particular technology might afford (or perceived to be affording) to different people, in different circumstances. This is particularly important when considering AI technologies, since these often result in behaviour, outcomes and reactions which might be unintended by its designers. To be more specific, we will focus our discussion on a specific type of technological affordances called **Learning Affordances**. So in our context, we would define a learning affordance as **a learning-related ability a user perceives to be achievable as a result of interacting with a particular technology**.

The term 'affordance' [21] was used [22] as a way to characterise the perceived value of an object (a learning technology in our case) to the user, in addition to its actual value. This definition has made the concept of affordances very popular with instructional designers and other educational technology designers. Educational researchers considered the affordance of mobile technologies [23, 24, 25], affordances of general information and communication technologies [26, 27], blogs [28], 3D virtual worlds [29] and wearable technologies [30]. Kirschner et al. [31] made a distinction between technological affordances, social affordances and educational affordances. However, this distinction was met with some criticisms because it is very often hard to make [30].

The Technology Affordances and Constraints Theory (TACT) [32] has shed some light on the significance of **limitations** (or constraints) imposed by technologies in addition to their **affordances**. If a **technology affordance** refers to a potential action that a user with a particular purpose can do with a technology, then a **technology constraint** refers to ways in which the user could be held back from fulfilling a particular goal when using the same technology. Again, as affordances were not meant to be directly associated with certain technological features, so were limitations. As affordances can vary by user and context, so do limitations. This distinction is helpful in explaining the different subjective learning experiences of learners who are equipped with varying abilities, levels of knowledge, technological literacy, data literacy and external contexts.

For example, think of an ML model that predicts who will drop out of school. It is possible that one teacher could perceive this system's affordance as identifying which **characteristics** of students might be important in that prediction (for example, attendance). A second teacher might be more focused on their use of the prediction itself, for example, in setting up early interventions for those students who are highly predicted to drop out. A third teacher might be influenced by the fact that students with English as a second language seem to have a higher tendency to drop out, therefore they might be biased (even unintentionally) to view students with non-native English differently.

Figure 1.5 illustrates the first three steps we have laid out until now: (1) the differential analysis of human and AI skill sets; (2) how to bring them together; and (3) identify affordances and constraints of different users.

Once we have identified these three aspects of the AI system, we are ready to take the fourth step into evaluating our technology in our own specific learning context.

STEP 4: EVALUATING THE IMPACT OF AI SYSTEMS IN SPECIFIC EDUCATIONAL SETTINGS

As educators, instructional designers, decision-makers, users or developers of AI systems in education, one of our goals is to evaluate the impact of a certain technology on our specific learning and teaching practices. What might be effective to one class might be

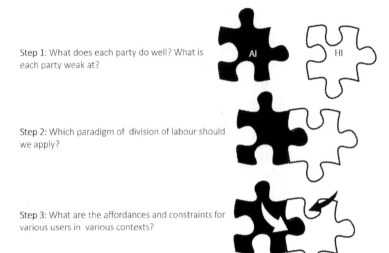

Step 1: What does each party do well? What is each party weak at?

Step 2: Which paradigm of division of labour should we apply?

Step 3: What are the affordances and constraints for various users in various contexts?

Figure 1.5 Step 1: differential analysis of human and AI skills set; Step 2: how to bring them together; Step 3: identify affordances and constraints of different users.

completely inappropriate for another. Once we have mapped the human and AI's skill sets, evaluated their interaction with each other and identified our technology's affordances and constraints, it is time to integrate the technology into the classroom effectively, which is what we will focus on in Step 4.

The affordances of traditional educational technologies seem very straightforward: a pencil is for writing, a microscope is for viewing small objects, whiteboards and reusable blackboards and are used for writing in front of a classroom. These affordances are very clear to their users and are rarely challenged or changed [20]. In contrast, educational digital technologies, and especially AI-based technologies, are characterised by a wide span of affordances and constraints. AI's affordances are diverse, highly contextual and frequently changing and are often opaque (in the sense that it might be difficult to be clear about how they operate). Add to this the already ill-defined nature of teaching and learning in the digital world, and you get a technology that offers tremendous potential to assist but is still far from being seamless.

Technology (and particularly AI) is a moving target and is far from being unbiased, neutral or able to be securely deployed without continuous evaluation and regulation. It was for this reason that frameworks were developed which are designed to assist teachers in integrating educational technology into their classrooms. We briefly present two of them here, SAMR and TPACK, and illustrate how they may be applied to the intricacies of AI.

SAMR (SUBSTITUTION, AUGMENTATION, MODIFICATION, REDEFINITION)

The <u>SAMR framework</u> was devised by Puentedura, who identified four levels of classroom technology integration [33]: Substitution and Augmentation (both of which are considered in the model to play a role of enhancing education) and Modification and Redefinition (which are considered to transform education, rather than just enhance education). SAMR looks at technology integration as a journey, beginning with the most basic form of technology integration (Substitution) and ending with what it views as potentially the most valuable form of technology integration (Redefinition).

For example, consider the task of reading from a textbook for the purpose of comprehension or drawing a picture for the purpose of expressing oneself. The Substitution phase could be using a digital textbook or digital painting software. This would afford the pupils to easily use exactly the same resource at home and in the classroom, and ensure that it can be backed up. The Augmentation phase might involve adding a text-to-speech and search functionality or in the drawing example – integrating an image search engine to find similar images on the web. This again will add some affordances (such as accessibility or external inspiration) as well as some constraints. Puentedura considers these two phases to be using technology for the purpose of enhancement and not transformation, as the task has not been significantly affected by the technology. Moving the model towards transforming the learning task, the Modification phase entails a significant task redesign. It might include adding image classification functionality to the drawing task, where an AI agent would suggest to the artist what it 'sees' in their image and, by that, affording them the opportunity of reflecting and adding an external point of view. However, this technology would also impose some constraints, as it might 'fence in' the artist's imagination and pose artificial external limitations. In the Redefinition phase, the drawing task could be supported by a robot 'collaborator', for example, which would 'generate' some drawings itself as suggestions to the human artist. In the textbook example, an adaptive technology could be added, suggesting a different sequence of reading to each student, and tailoring supporting materials to their ability.

SAMR is a useful model, and its primary strength is in its simplicity. However, we argue that it is this simplicity that also limits it. First, the basic assumption underlying SAMR is the view of a linear progression from substitution to augmentation to modification to redefinition. However, as we discussed in Step 2, we cannot assume that either substitution or augmentation is not in fact our ultimate goal, nor that redefining learning **is** our goal. Second, SAMR is very focused on the result of the technology integration, and less on the process and what can be learned from it, which in our mind is equally important. Third, it does not emphasise the pedagogical objective enough as the driver of technology integration. SAMR is very focused on the technology and its affordances. However, in reality, we believe pedagogy and the knowledge domain should be the drivers of the technology integration process, and not the other way around. For these reasons, we also mention an alternative evaluation framework called TPACK.

TPACK (TECHNOLOGICAL, PEDAGOGICAL AND CONTENT KNOWLEDGE)

When planning technology integration into the classroom, TPACK [35] forces you to focus on three components: pedagogy, content and technology, along with the relationships between them. TPACK

[34] is designed to identify a technology-based instructional strategy, based on a view of teaching as an interactional model between what teachers know, how they apply what they know and the unique context of their classroom.

Content knowledge (CK) refers to teachers' knowledge about the subject matter, including its concepts, theories, ideas and evidence. **Pedagogical knowledge (PK)** refers to teachers' knowledge about the processes, practices or methods of teaching and learning, including their educational purposes, values and aims. **Technological knowledge (TK)** refers to the teachers' understanding of how to apply information technologies productively and their ability to critically evaluate the way it could assist (or impede) the achievement of their pedagogical goals.

We contend that there is a fourth component needed for this framework to reach its potential, which is **Data Knowledge (DK)** (added into the lower side of Figure 1.6). AI educational technologies (but also all other forms of educational technology) cannot be evaluated without systematically collecting, analysing and reflecting on the evidence about the efficacy of those technologies, how they are actually being used (and therefore their intended and unintended affordances) and how different students are operating within them. The whole goal of the TPACK model is to devise an optimal instructional strategy. How would teachers know it is indeed optimal without collecting data about it? The **Data Knowledge component** would include the data produced by the technology itself as well as from other sources that could generate any evidence about the quality of the teaching and learning supported by this technology (Figure 1.6).

One of the strengths of the TPACK evaluation model is its recognition of the complex relationships between its components. For example, technological affordances often make a significant impact on the content knowledge, both metaphorically and practically. In a similar way, data, as well as AI models, have direct effects on pedagogy, content and technology [36]. TPCA(D)K (Technological, Pedagogical, Content and Data Knowledge), therefore, represents an emergent form of knowledge that combines the four components, as well as the interactions among them, in a specific context.

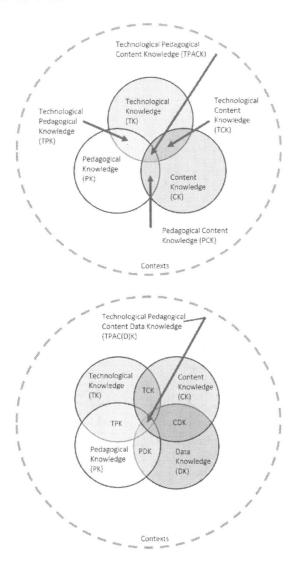

Figure 1.6 Left – TPACK model – the image was reproduced with permission of the publisher, © 2012 by tpack.org [35]; right – TPAC(D)K – our modification, adding the data component.

As an example of how TPCA(D)K can be used, we cite a scenario entitled 'K-6 Literacy Activity Types Classroom Example: The Writing Process' written by Harris et al. [37]. The scenario describes a teacher designing a *"Writer's Workshop approach in his third-grade classroom to teach writing composition and skills. His third-grade students work independently, following each stage of the writing process – prewriting, drafting, revising, editing, and publishing – to compose numerous stories throughout the school year"*.

The **prewriting** portion of this scenario is presented below as an example. We have suggested some additions in **bold font** to make it more AI-related. We have proposed some additions to the underlined font in order to account for the addition of the Data component to the classical TPACK model.

> *During the prewriting stage, students begin to brainstorm their story ideas using a word processor. Students type as many topics as they can think of to write about and save their documents, adding to their lists each week. Each student begins a new story by choosing a topic from that list, then creates a concept map using Inspiration. Each student's concept map helps her to visualize her ideas, illustrating various connections and relationships made while brainstorming the topic* [37].
> **A computer program will be used to analyse each concept map and suggest extensions and new relationships based on semantic proximity.** Mr Smith will collect data on the students' engagement with the concept maps so that he can construct meaningful feedback for each student. For example, he will use data about the connections made in the concept maps as an indicator to the students ability to integrate knowledge topics and infer, to identify misconceptions and more.

STEP 5: CLOSING THE CYCLE ... AND ITERATING BACK

As educators and learners, we all know that a learning process is rarely linear and that it certainly never ends. This is also how we suggest viewing our five-step framework. The five steps would therefore entail collecting the evidence from the fourth step to reflect upon what works, what did not work and then to iterate back to any of the four phases to learn again.

REFERENCES

1. Greenwood, V. (2017, November 10). The invention of cake mix nearly foundered – but when manufacturers made a counter-intuitive change to their simple recipe, sales boomed. BBC. https://www.bbc.com/future/article/20171027-the-magic-cakes-that-come-from-a-packet

2. Nass, C., & Yen, C. (2010). *The man who lied to his laptop: What we can learn about ourselves from our machines.* Penguin, New York, US.

3. Tversky, A., & Kahneman, D. (1974). Judgment under uncertainty: Heuristics and biases. *Science, 185*(4157), 1124–1131.

4. Russel, S., & Norvig, P. (2016). *Artificial Intelligence: A modern approach.* Malaysia: Pearson Education Limited. doi:10.1017/S0269888900007724

5. Luckin, R. (2018). *Machine learning and Human Intelligence: The future of education for the 21st century.* UCL IOE Press, London, UK.

6. Weizenbaum, J. (1966). ELIZA – a computer program for the study of natural language communication between man and machine. *Communications of the ACM, 9*(1), 36–45.

7. Güzeldere, G., & Franchi, S. (1995). Dialogues with colorful "personalities" of early AI. *Stanford Humanities Review, 4*(2), 161–169.

8. Salmons, J. (2019). *Learning to collaborate, collaborating to learn: Engaging students in the classroom and online.* Stylus Publishing, LLC, Sterling, US.

9. Wegner, D. M. (1987). Transactive memory: A contemporary analysis of the group mind. In Brian Mullen and George R. Goethals (eds.), *Theories of group behavior* (pp. 185–208). New York, US: Springer.

10. Liang, D. W., Moreland, R., & Argote, L. (1995). Group versus individual training and group performance: The mediating role of transactive memory. *Personality and Social Psychology Bulletin, 21*(4), 384–393.

11. Cook, M. B., & Smallman, H. S. (2008). Human factors of the confirmation bias in intelligence analysis: Decision support from graphical evidence landscapes. *Human Factors, 50*(5), 745–754.

12. Van den Hoven, J., Vermaas, P. E., & Van de Poel, I. (Eds.). (2015). *Handbook of ethics, values, and technological design: Sources, theory, values and application domains.* Dordrecht: Springer Netherlands.

13. Akata, Z., Balliet, D., De Rijke, M., Dignum, F., Dignum, V., Eiben, G., Fokkens, A., Grossi, D., Hindriks, K., Hoos, H., & Hung, H. (2020). A research agenda for hybrid intelligence: Augmenting human intellect with collaborative, adaptive, responsible, and explainable Artificial Intelligence. *Computer*, 53(8), 18–28.

14. Hutchins, E. (2001). Distributed cognition. In J. S. Neil & B. B. Paul (Eds.), *The international encyclopedia of the social and behavioral sciences* (pp. 2068 –2072). Oxford: Pergamon Press.

15. Dellermann, D., Calma, A., Lipusch, N., Weber, T., Weigel, S., & Ebel, P. (2019). The future of human-AI collaboration: a taxonomy of design knowledge for hybrid intelligence systems. In Proceedings of the 52nd Hawaii *International Conference on System Sciences*.

16. Neef, M. (2006, January). A taxonomy of human-agent team collaborations. In Proceedings of the 18th BeNeLux *Conference on Artificial Intelligence* (BNAIC), Namur, Belgium (pp. 245–250).

17. Rauschert, I., Agrawal, P., Sharma, R., Fuhrmann, S., Brewer, I., & MacEachren, A. (2002, November). Designing a human-centered, multimodal GIS interface to support emergency management. In Proceedings of the 10th *ACM international symposium on Advances in geographic information systems* (pp. 119–124).

18. De Graaf, M. M., & Malle, B. F. (2017, October). How people explain action (and autonomous intelligent systems should too). In 2017 AAAI Fall Symposium Series.

19. Norman, D. A. (1988). *The psychology of everyday things.* New York: Basic Books.

20. Koehler, M., & Mishra, P. (2009). What is technological pedagogical content knowledge (TPACK)? *Contemporary issues in technology and teacher education,* 9(1), 60–70.

21. Gibson, J. (1977). The theory of affordances. In R. E. Shaw & J. Bransford (eds.), *Perceiving, acting, and knowing.* Lawrence Erlbaum Associates, Hillsdale, NJ.

22. Norman, D. A. (1999). Affordance, conventions, and design. *Interactions,* 6(3), 38–43.

23. Churchill, D., & Churchill, N. (2008). Educational affordances of PDAs: A study of a teacher's exploration of this technology. *Computers & Education,* 50(4), 1439–1450.

24. Cochrane, T., & Bateman, R. (2010). Smartphones give you wings: Pedagogical affordances of mobile Web 2.0. *Australasian Journal of Educational Technology,* 26(1), 1–14.

25. Klopfer, E., & Squire, K. (2008). Environmental detectives — the development of an augmented reality platform for environmental simulations. *Educational Technology Research and Development*, 56(2), 203–228.

26. Bower, M. (2008). Affordance analysis–matching learning tasks with learning technologies. *Educational Media International*, 45(1), 3–15.

27. Conole, G., & Dyke, M. (2004). What are the affordances of information and communication technologies? *Association for Learning Technology Journal*, 12(2), 113–124.

28. Deng, L., & Yuen, A. H. K. (2011). Towards a framework for educational affordances of blogs. *Computers & Education*, 56(2), 441–451.

29. Dalgarno, B., & Lee, M. J. W. (2010). What are the learning affordances of 3-D virtual environments? *British Journal of Educational Technology*, 40(6), 10–32.

30. Bower, M., & Sturman, D. (2015). What are the educational affordances of wearable technologies? *Computers & Education*, 88, 343–353.

31. Kirschner, P., Strijbos, J.-W., Kreijns, K., & Beers, P. J. (2004). Designing electronic collaborative learning environments. *Educational Technology Research & Development*, 52(3), 47–66.

32. Majchrzak, A. & Markus, L. (2013). Technology affordances and constraints in management information systems (MIS). In E. Kessler (Ed.), *Encyclopedia of management theory*. Thousand Oaks: Sage Publications.

33. Puentedura, R. (2006). Transformation, technology, and education [Blog post]. Retrieved from http://hippasus.com/resources/tte/.

34. Mishra, P., & Koehler, M. J. (2006). Technological pedagogical content knowledge: A framework for integrating technology in teachers' knowledge. *Teachers College Record*, 108(6), 1017–1054.

35. TPACK ORG. http://tpack.org

36. Kent, Carmel, Muhammad Ali Chaudhry, Mutlu Cukurova, Ibrahim Bashir, Hannah Pickard, Chris Jenkins, Benedict du Boulay, Anissa Moeini, and Rosemary Luckin. "Machine Learning Models and Their Development Process as Learning Affordances for Humans." In *International Conference on Artificial Intelligence in Education*, pp. 228–240. Springer, Cham, 2021.

37. Harris, J., Hofer, M., Blanchard, M., Grandgenett, N., Schmidt, D., Van Olphen, M., & Young, C. (2010). "Grounded" technology integration: Instructional planning using curriculum-based activity type taxonomies. *Journal of Technology and Teacher Education*, 18(4), 573–605.

2

AI AS A LEARNER

HOW CAN AI HELP ME LEARN THINGS THAT I DID NOT UNDERSTAND BEFORE?

Figure 2.1 How can AI help me learn things that I did not understand before? Illustrated by Yael Toiber Kent.

Synopsis: This chapter explains how you can use AI to help you to get to grips with something you don't yet fully understand. A commonly reported experience of teachers is that they only really started to understand a topic or skill once they tried to teach it. There are two reasons for this. First, teaching requires teachers to externalise their understanding, e.g. through speaking, writing or illustrating, and such an externalisation can then be examined by the teachers as to its adequacy and coherence. Second, the questions and other

DOI: 10.1201/9781003194545-2

reactions of the learners to what the teacher has externalised may well raise issues that the teacher had not examined carefully enough, leading to a better quality externalisation. This chapter explores the idea of providing the human learner with an artificial pupil (the AI learner) that they have to teach and, in so doing, come to understand some ideas or develop some skills. This chapter also covers the learner's side of this equation and discusses the differences between human learning and artificial learning.

BACKGROUND

There are two broad ways that AI as 'a learner' can be referred to in education: (i) as a contrast to human learners and (ii) as a pupil to the human learner.

AS A CONTRAST TO HUMAN LEARNERS

The first way relates back to Chapter 1 in which the differences between human intelligence and artificial intelligence are described. There are many pressures within the UK school curriculum to learn and memorise facts, an activity that artificial intelligence is really good at, where what is needed is the growth of understanding and wisdom, which human intelligence can become good at. By educating human learners about the different ways that humans and computers learn and about the differences between human and artificial intelligence we have a chance to help human learners reclaim and celebrate what they are more naturally good at. One significant difference between human learners and computer learners lies in their different **metacognitive capabilities** [1]. That is, humans can reflect on their own learning, checking how much they have understood, where the gaps are and can direct their engagement and attention to make their learning more effective. One of the capabilities that start to develop at school is precisely this metacognitive reflection and regulation, together with some skills that can be brought into play such as looking things up, asking someone more expert and so on.

For those who go on to university this capability and its associated skills develop further with many universities reasonably claiming that their graduates have 'learned how to learn'.

We are not arguing that there is no place for memorisation and rote learning. For example, being able to do mental arithmetic based on rote learning of the times tables is useful in that it offers an easy way for someone to check the accuracy of a calculation and perhaps more importantly it offers a way for someone to have a rough sense of what size the answer should be. This memorisation ability is used as a 'mental shortcut' and can be used to validate an answer arrived at by using a calculator or similar device where miskeying would otherwise go unnoticed.

AS A PUPIL TO THE HUMAN LEARNER

A commonly reported experience is that one only really starts to understand a topic or skill once one has tried to teach it. There are two reasons for this. First, teaching requires one to externalise one's understanding, e.g. through speaking, writing or illustrating, and one can then examine such an externalisation as to its adequacy and coherence. Second, the questions and other reactions of others to what one has externalised may well raise issues that one had not examined carefully enough, leading to a better quality externalisation.

So, the second way that AI as 'a learner' can be used in education is by providing the human learner with such an AI learner, either as a comparative model of learning (see above), or as a means for the human learner to act **as a teacher** to that AI learner. The idea behind this is that the human learner gradually builds up some skill or understanding, piece by piece, by instructing the AI learner and can then test how well the AI learner is then able to perform the skill or demonstrate its understanding. In the early stages the AI learner will get things wrong, and the human learner will need to reflect on what he or she has taught the AI learner and make adjustments to it. So there is a cycle of building, checking and modifying what has been taught. What has been taught will have been externalised and open to reflection and modification and it is this process that helps the human learner master what they have tried to teach. Most teachers have experienced an increase in their own understanding as a result of trying to teach others.

In order to explain how AI can act as a learner for a human student, it is necessary to say a little about how educational technology systems are able to provide this capability. To do this, we need to say something about the architecture of such systems and in particular about their interfaces to the human learner.

THE ARCHITECTURE OF AIED SYSTEMS

In Chapter 1 we introduced the idea of an evaluative framework for judging how well a piece of educational AI-based technology works in practice. At the heart of step four of this framework was the TPACK model (or our suggested extension, the TPCA(D)K model – Technological, Pedagogical, Content and Data Knowledge). Two of the TPACK's components are the teacher's content knowledge and pedagogical knowledge. TPACK provides a way to examine technology-based educational systems and interventions. In this chapter, we focus on the architecture and main components of the educational systems that embody artificial intelligence. We will refer to them generically as AIED systems. So while TPACK considered the teacher's knowledge in the context of integrating the technology in the actual learning and teaching context, here we consider the different kinds of knowledge embedded in the technology itself. Unsurprisingly, there are some similarities to teachers' knowledge already described.

As briefly outlined in the Introduction to this book, it is usual to divide the conceptual architecture of AIED systems into four components (see Figure I.2 in the Introduction). A conceptual architecture is an **idealised** division of a technological system into separate but intercommunicating components. An actual system will be made up of a complex set of programs that may well be organised in a very different way, but which in broad terms behave as implied by the conceptual architecture. The first component is the system's <u>domain knowledge</u>, i.e. what the system knows about the area to be taught and this corresponds to the teacher's content knowledge in the TPACK evaluative model. The second component is the <u>learner model</u>. This corresponds to what the system knows about the learner, i.e. what the learner understands and his or her skills. This model will change over time as the learner learns. The third component is the <u>pedagogical model</u>, i.e. the rules which guide how it interacts with the learner. This corresponds to the teacher's pedagogical knowledge in the TPACK model. The fourth component of the AIED conceptual architecture is the <u>interface</u>, which does not have a parallel in TPACK, and is about the means through which the learner and the system can communicate.

THE INTERFACE BETWEEN THE LEARNER AND THE SYSTEM

The **interface** provides the means through which the human learner can communicate with the system to build a model of what is to be learnt, view it, modify it and check how well it performs. Different kinds of interface enable different kinds of concepts to be more readily expressed than others. For example, a word-processing interface is rather better for writing a thank-you letter than a spreadsheet interface, though you could use a spreadsheet if you were minded to. Likewise, a spreadsheet interface is much better than a word-processing interface for doing your accounts. The interfaces of these two kinds of system, how they look on your screen and what you can do in those interfaces are very different. In other words they have different potential affordances, as described in Chapter 1. According to the Cambridge Dictionary, an affordance is "*a use or purpose that a thing can have, that people notice as part of the way they see or experience it. In design, perceived affordance is important — that is, our implicit understanding of how to interact with an object*".

Both the word-processing and spreadsheet interfaces are visible and manipulable representations of otherwise hidden internal structures i.e. a model of your letter or a model of your finances. A change that you make through the interface e.g. correcting a misspelling is reflected in the model of the letter. In a similar way, changing a number in a column in a spreadsheet may well change a number in some other cell that you have labelled as 'total' because the internal mechanisms have recomputed the sum of the numbers in the column via the underlying model. You can think of the interface as the means of communication between the user and the system.

THE DOMAIN MODEL

The second component is a, largely hidden, model of the domain that can be used to check how well the model developed by the human learner actually performs. For example, if the human learner were building a model of an ecological system (see later), then there needs to be a way to determine whether the model being built is correct, or partially correct or plain wrong, and to point out discrepancies between what has been built and what should have been built. This internal model of the ecosystem represents an expert view of the ecology. It could be displayed through the interface, but that would rather undermine the whole point, which is to get the learner to build the model.

THE LEARNER MODEL

The learner model holds information about the learner: how they are progressing, what they know, what they can do and so on. In the case of a human learner teaching the system, a large part of what the learner knows is expressed by the learner's actions applied through the interface. So if the learner teaches the system about how to do something correctly, it's a reasonable assumption that the learner knows how to do it, though it might be a fluke. If the learner teaches the system something that is incorrect, it's a reasonable assumption that the learner does not understand it, although it may just be a slip. If the learner omits to teach the system something important, it's not clear without other evidence whether the learner knows it and just did not teach it or does not know it at all.

Other useful information gathered in the learner model would also include how the learner uses the system, makes use of the help facilities and approaches the task of teaching. This information can be used by the system to offer help and advice via the pedagogical model.

THE PEDAGOGICAL MODEL

The fourth component that is needed is a pedagogical model. This model would determine what kinds of reactions the system would have at different stages of the building, what feedback should be provided if there are mistakes and what hints, help and scaffolding should be offered at different times. Hints, help and scaffolding might be provided at the level of the topic (e.g. an ecological system) but also might be at a meta-level concerning the way that the human learner is going about the business of teaching the AI learner.

EXAMPLES

a) *Human learners teaching an AI learner*

While it is commonly expected that an AIED system will provide the functionality of a tutor/teacher/mentor to help the human student learn, there has also been a long history of providing the functionality of a peer or companion [2]. In this chapter, we explore the value of the peer or companion being taught by the human learner. For a review of the wide variety of roles that pedagogical agents can play, see for example [3].

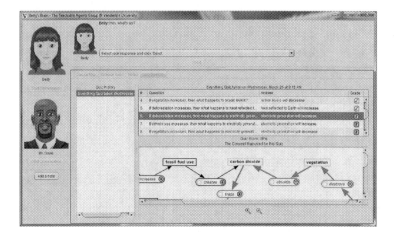

Figure 2.2 Interface to Betty's Brain [4].

A classic example of this way of learning is called Betty's Brain (see Figure 2.2) [4, 5]. In this system, the human learner has access to online materials about a topic, ecology, for example. The learner is expected to read these materials and use the interface to start to draw a <u>concept map</u> that captures some of the ecological processes involved, such as the production of oxygen and carbon dioxide. The concept map is built from a menu of nodes and arrows, where the arrows link nodes together indicating some kind of causal process, e.g. fossil fuel use produces carbon dioxide.

The initial concept map is empty and is gradually filled out by the human learner. At any time, the learner can ask for their concept map to be tested for accuracy and completeness. The system is able to track the reasoning implicit in the concept map, see whether it is accurate and provide appropriate feedback if it is not. The 'cover story' for the educational interaction is that the concept map is an externalisation of the understanding of a simulated student, Betty, hence 'Betty's Brain'. So, the human student is trying to teach Betty and if Betty's concept map is not accurate, it does not reflect directly on the human student's capability, i.e. Betty failed her test, not the human student.

There is also a simulated teacher in the system, Mr Davis, who offers metacognitive advice to the human student, such as pointing her to the online materials if she does not seem to be using them and reminding her that offering a concept map for a second test without making any change to it will necessarily generate the same set of issues to be fixed and not really help her learning. Mr Davis' interventions and responses are driven by the pedagogical model in the system.

In the earlier days of AIED, one of our students built a system (LECOBA) for the human learner (at the undergraduate level) to teach a pedagogical agent about Boolean algebra [6]. The human student selected rule parts from a menu to build rules that solved problems in Boolean algebra. This process was similar to the way a human learner would select nodes and links in Betty's Brain to build a model of an ecological system. If the rules built were correct, the problems would be solved correctly. If the rules built were wrong, the problems would not be solved and the rules would need to be adjusted.

In an evaluation of LECOBA, two aspects of the design of LECOBA were found to be much disliked by the human students. There was a mechanism in the simulated student that caused it to not always correctly make use of the rules it had been taught and there was also a mechanism that simulated human forgetfulness in that the simulated student was designed to occasionally forget what it had been taught. These two mechanisms were introduced to make the simulated student behave in a more human-like way. The human students found this human-like behaviour in the simulated student very frustrating, not least because it seemed to violate their sense that computers don't forget stuff, and if they are told how to do something, they will do it just as instructed. While this can easily be written off as a poor design decision, it could also have been a springboard for a discussion of the differences between human learning/intelligence and artificial learning/intelligence.

b)   *Teachers teaching an AI learner*

It's not just students who can benefit from working with AI as a learner: teachers can too. An interesting early AIED paper [7] describes different ways that simulated students can be used, both for use by human learners (as described above) **and** by human teachers. When a teacher is developing and exploring different ways of teaching a topic, they can base their initial lesson plan on experience and perhaps try it out with some students to see how well it works in practice and then modify it as needs be. AI can also be used to provide the teacher with a class of simulated students with whom the human teacher can try out different ways of tackling a topic to see which way works best, or which way causes particular problems that need to be fixed.

In this kind of application, the crucial component is that there is an AI model of the simulated student and of the way that the simulated student learns. Such a model needs to be psychologically plausible so that both successful learning and unsuccessful learning in the simulated student match the kinds of successful learning and unsuccessful learning in human students.

A more recent adaptation of the same idea is to be found in [8]. They describe using a system called SimStudent as a way to help novice human authors build intelligent tutoring systems without having to learn a great deal of programming. In other words, they were using SimStudent as an "*authoring system*". They explain that

> in the context of Authoring by Tutoring, the author interactively tutors SimStudent by posing problems to SimStudent, providing feedback on the steps performed by SimStudent, and also demonstrating steps as a response to SimStudent's hint requests when SimStudent cannot perform steps correctly [8].

Again the success or otherwise of this approach depends largely on the psychological plausibility of the model of learning embedded in SimStudent. While the model is cognitively plausible, it is simulating a fully engaged, motivated and attentive student – such conditions do not always obtain in real classrooms.

EVALUATION USING THE FRAMEWORK

In this section, we develop the idea of how you might evaluate tools that use AI as a learner, taking Betty's Brain and LECOBA as particular examples of this use of AI.

STEP 1: WHAT WE ARE GOOD AT, WHAT ARE MACHINES GOOD AT?

The idea of learning by teaching is an old one, though prior to AI it was an activity between people. One example is *"reciprocal teaching"* where two or more learners take it in turn to teach each other [9]. Indeed, human teachers routinely ask learners to explain back some concept or demonstrate some skill, almost as if the teacher did not already understand them, as a device to get learners to reflect on what they know or can do.

Being able to offload this task onto an AI learner is a way for the human teacher to use her time more efficiently, so long as she can be confident that the AI learner has been designed in such a way as to be likely to be helpful. In any case, she will need both to introduce the AI learner and how to interact with it prior to the human learner's session with it, as well as debrief the human learner after the session to get a sense of how effective that session has been. The extra capabilities that the AI learner brings to this use of AI are that (i) it is endlessly patient as the human learner tries out different ideas, (ii) it offers a means for the human learner to set out what they know in a visible and editable form and (iii) the AI learner can demonstrate both the correct and incorrect aspects of the description that the human learner has built.

STEP 2: HOW CAN HUMANS AND MACHINES WORK TOGETHER?

We do not see the technology of 'AI as a learner' as being a technology that can readily be used without some kind of assistance from a human teacher or another responsible person. There will be many times when the human learner will misunderstand what they are supposed to do and how they are supposed to do it that the inbuilt help system cannot fix. Also the activity with the AI learner will also need to be framed by the human teacher so as to make it make sense to and motivate the human learner in the wider context of that class or sequence of classes.

The human teacher may determine that the AI learner should be used by pairs or groups of human learners rather than one-to-one using her human insight into her students that the AI learner just will not have. In all, we see this as a helpful technology that needs to be 'orchestrated' by a human teacher (see Chapter 4). To that extent, we can see that this kind of interaction is a Human AI Transactive Collaboration with a well-defined division of labour, i.e. Paradigm 4 in the Introduction to this book.

STEP 3: ON AFFORDANCES AND CONSTRAINTS OF AI IN LEARNING AND TEACHING

Let us consider the characteristics of an AI learner that are needed to make it successful.

1. Clearly, it needs an interface within which the human learner can create the knowledge or skill in question and this needs to be appropriate for the age, ability and background of the human learner.
2. There also needs to be a way that the human learner can cause the AI learner to behave, based on what it has been taught: in the case of Betty's Brain, this is to take a test on ecology and in the case of LECOBA this is to solve Boolean algebra problems.
3. The individual components out of which knowledge or skill is described need to be understandable to the human learner. In the case of the nodes and arrows of Betty's Brain, an evaluation showed that some learners did not understand the logic embedded in the arrows and how they could be chained together to draw a conclusion between two nodes separated by other nodes in the concept map [4].
4. Ideally, the AI learner system needs the capability of offering help to the human learners if they are not making progress in doing their teaching. There is a tension here in that the AI learner knows nothing initially other than the meaning of the individual knowledge or skill components, and yet it should be

able to give advice. This is normally dealt with by introducing another agent on the screen, a teacher, Mr Davis, in the case of Betty's Brain.

STEP 4: HOW CAN THIS AI TECHNOLOGY BE INTEGRATED INTO THE CLASSROOM?

While we have described AI as a learner to just a single human learner, there is no reason why a small group of learners might not work together with the AI learner. From the teacher's point of view, the main tasks are setting expectations and motivating those who are going to use the technology, helping those who get stuck or lost while using the technology, and after the event getting the users to reflect and explain what they have learnt from the experience. Ideally, the teacher will need some technical assistance to ensure that the technology is functioning properly too.

Using the TPCA(D)K model introduced in Chapter 1, we can see that the content knowledge of an 'AI as a learner' system largely lies in the design of the low-level components (e.g. nodes and arrows in Betty's Brain) that are made available to the human learners to build their descriptions and in design of the means available to test the quality of those descriptions.

The pedagogical knowledge largely lies in the rules that govern the way that the system tracks the manner in which the learner is building and testing descriptions it might also lie in the interventions the system takes should the human learner's progress in building and testing seem to be ineffective.

The technological knowledge lies largely in the quality of the interface and the degree to which it supports or hinders productive activity by the human learner.

Finally, the data knowledge of the system lies largely in what data is stored during a session to enable the pedagogical rules to work at all. It also lies in the data that it stores between sessions in order to (i) enable the same learner to carry on from where she left off on the next session; and (ii) provide the human teacher with some sense of how well the session went so that she can conduct her debrief of the human learner.

STEP 5: REFLECT AND ITERATE

It is rare that an educational system works as expected when first tried out in authentic settings, which is why iterating to reflect and improve is an inherent part of the process.

We already indicated earlier that one of the design decisions in LECOBA, namely having the simulated student forget or misunderstand things it was taught, was not liked by the human learners who taught it.

There have been various evaluations of Betty's Brain [4]. One finding was that some learners were not good at understanding or tracing along the arrows in the conceptual map, e.g. that increased sunlight helps plants grow which increases dissolved oxygen, which in its turn increases bacteria. So later versions of the system added in features to tutor on that issue.

REFERENCES

1. Azevedo, R., & Aleven, V. (Eds.). (2013). *International handbook of metacognition and learning technologies*. Springer International Handbooks of Education. Springer.

2. Chan, T.-W., & Baskin, A. B. (1990). Learning companion systems. In C. Frasson and G. Gauthier (eds.), *Intelligent tutoring systems: At the crossroads of Artificial Intelligence and education* (pp. 6–33). Norwood, New Jersey: Ablex.

3. Kim, Y., & Baylor, A. L. (2016). Research-based design of pedagogical agent roles: A review, progress, and recommendations. *International Journal of Artificial Intelligence in Education*, 26(1), 160–169.

4. Biswas, G., Segedy, J. R., & Bunchongchit, K. (2016). From design to implementation to practice a learning by teaching system: Betty's Brain. *International Journal of Artificial Intelligence in Education*, 26(1), 350–364.

5. Leelawong, K., & Biswas, G. (2008). Designing learning by teaching agents: The Betty's Brain System. *International Journal of Artificial Intelligence in Education*, 18(3), 181–208.

6. Uresti, J. A. R., & du Boulay, B. (2004). Expertise, motivation and teaching in learning companion systems. *International Journal of Artificial Intelligence in Education*, 14(2), 193–231.

7. VanLehn, K., Ohlsson, S., & Nason, R. (1994). Applications of simulated students. *Journal of Artificial Intelligence in Education*, 5(2), 135–175.

8. Matsuda, N., Cohen, W. W., & Koedinger, K. R. (2015). Teaching the teacher: Tutoring SimStudent leads to more effective cognitive tutor authoring. *International Journal of Artificial Intelligence in Education*, 25(1), 1–34.

9. Palincsar, A. S., & Brown, A. L. (1984). Reciprocal teaching of comprehension-fostering and comprehension-monitoring activities. *Cognition and Instruction*, 1(2), 117–175.

3

AI AS A TUTOR

HOW CAN AI TUTOR ME ABOUT STUFF?

Figure 3.1 How can AI tutor me about stuff? Illustrated by Yael Toiber Kent.

Synopsis: This chapter explains how AI can tutor new ideas and how to do new things. We use the word 'tutor' in the title of this chapter rather than the word 'teacher' because the focus in this chapter is on one-to-one interactions, and teaching involves other activities too, such as classroom management. However, we have used both words

DOI: 10.1201/9781003194545-3

largely interchangeably within the chapter. In many ways, the classic use of AI has been the building of artificial tutors aimed at teaching skills and concepts. The very phrase 'intelligent tutoring systems' has come to be synonymous with AIED, although originally it referred to a particular AI-based tutoring style. This style involved one-to-one tutoring a problem-solving skill, such as programming, by monitoring the learner step by step and intervening with help and advice immediately that the learner seemed to be veering off a good path to a solution.

This chapter looks at what effective human tutoring is about and then provides some background from the history of AI in education to help understand its current state. The current state is illustrated through three example systems. The first is a tutor that concentrates on the content, the second is a tutor that not only concentrates on the content but also addresses issues around feelings and motivation, and the third is a tutor that not only concentrates on conceptual content but also offers advice about learning. The final section offers an evaluation using the framework set out in Chapter 1.

BACKGROUND

Various researchers have investigated what makes human tutoring effective [1]. They found that tutors who were reported to be effective by students were skilled in each of the following four tasks: (1) elaboration, e.g. helping the learner to understand a topic from a broader perspective; (2) directing the learning process, e.g. helping the learner to focus attention more effectively; (3) integration of knowledge, e.g. helping the learner to relate the new material to what they already know; and (4) stimulating interaction and individual accountability, e.g. helping the learner to discuss, collaborate and take charge of their own learning. They also found that tutors who focused on the learning process were perceived as more effective than those who focused on content. It has to be said that most AI-based tutors have tended to focus on individualising content but have not really been able to deal with points (1) and (3), as that requires them to understand enough about their learners to be able to **contextualise** the learning on an individual basis.

It might surprise you to read that the first AI-based teaching system, SCHOLAR, was built more than 50 years ago in 1970 to teach geography [2]. While there were computerised tutors before that time, they tended to be 'hard-wired' to teach a particular topic in a particular way which was hard to change without reprogramming the whole system. Moreover, they did not 'know or understand' the material that they taught so could not answer questions from their learners. SCHOLAR separated out its teaching strategy from its knowledge of geography, so in principle the system could teach the same geography but in a different manner by just changing the teaching method, or teach some other topic in the same way it taught geography just by changing the knowledge of the topic to be taught. To a great extent, this system embodied the AIED conceptual architecture of learner-facing systems described in Chapter 1, where content and pedagogy are modelled separately. In addition, the student could ask SCHOLAR questions about geography, as well as being quizzed by SCHOLAR, because its knowledge of geography was explicitly represented within the system.

Given the capabilities of computing in 1970, the interface was just textual and the system had only a limited ability to understand questions from the learner, as they had to be typed in a stylised fashion in simplified English. Things have changed a lot since 1970, when there was no Internet, no personal computers, no smartphones and limited graphical interfaces. A good contemporary contrast to SCHOLAR is the Enskill suite of language teachers [3]. These teachers help people learn a language, such as Spanish, Arabic or English, and help those in business learn how to express themselves clearly and with authority. The suite uses game-based methods to display a scene on the screen that contains one or more characters. The learner talks to the on-screen characters and the online characters talk back, so the language learning can be contextualised to expected situations. For example, one scene might be at a café to help the learner practice the skills of ordering food, or another at a tourist office to help the learner plan some travel and order tickets. The system is able to comment on the learner's language at many different levels, e.g. on the learner's choice of words, the pronunciation of those words, the grammar of what is said and its register (i.e. the tone and style of what is said). Having different scenarios for learning language and contextualising that learning is an example of an AIED conceptual architecture, in which the content is modelled or designed separately from the teaching strategy mentioned above. We return to the important issue of contextualising in the final section of this chapter.

EXAMPLES

As you might expect, there have been many tutoring and teaching systems for many different topics built since 1970. This is not the place to try to give a history of the subject, so we have been very selective in the examples we have chosen. In Chapter 2 we described one such tutoring system, called Betty's Brain, a system to help a student learn ecological concepts by teaching them to the computer in the form of a conceptual map [4].

In the rest of this section, we will describe an additional three tutoring systems. First will be a system for teaching algebra that sets the learner problems and then monitors, and potentially reacts to, every small step that the learner takes in solving those problems. It also aims towards mastery learning by carefully selecting the next problem for a learner depending on the progress so far. Second will be a system that also teaches mathematics but monitors the learners' behaviour to make inferences about their feelings and motivation. It uses this analysis both to select the next problem, as above, and to provide affective and motivational feedback, particularly based on the mindset work of Dweck [5]. Finally, we look at a system that is focused on helping the student learn how to learn and on fostering self-regulated learning behaviour, rather than on content.

KEEPING THE LEARNER ON TRACK

The Cognitive Tutors from Carnegie Learning are probably the best-known AI-based tutors for STEM subjects. For example, the Algebra Tutor [6, 7] teaches school-level algebraic problem-solving and monitors every step that the learner takes and not just the final answer to the problem. Systems that just check the final answer to a problem typically don't need much intelligence to do that and react with 'well done, that is correct', or 'sorry that is incorrect, try again'. Checking every step means that they can make helpful comments about how the learner is going about their problem-solving and not just about the outcome of that problem-solving. To do this they need to be able to distinguish good steps from bad steps, while allowing some latitude for learners to work in an individual fashion. These tutors have an explicit model of how to solve algebra problems that can be used as a comparison to how the learner is solving them. This model is derived from extensive prior work with learners so the tutors can recognise a wide variety of authentic ways for solving problems. However, it is always possible that a learner proceeds on a path that is not recognised as leading to a solution and the system will treat it as an error and so provide remedial help. These tutors also have an explicit model of mastery teaching that involves careful sequencing of problems based on the learner's individual progress through earlier problems.

There has been plenty of debate on the issue of whether such 'immediate feedback' to learners is effective or is annoyingly constraining or is positively unhelpful in terms of learning how to get out of problem-solving impasses. But it's perfectly clear that for many students at a particular level of growing expertise, this is an effective approach. The Algebra Tutor was evaluated in a multi-state experiment using matched schools [6, 7]. In each pair of schools one continued to teach algebra in the way they always had, while in the other school the Algebra Tutor was incorporated into their teaching. The experiment ran for two years, and in the second year those schools who had added the Algebra Tutor to their teaching produced learners who scored better on the math tests. We note that it took a year for the teachers in the schools using the Algebra Tutor to get used to having it and to develop ways to use it effectively in the context of their own style of teaching. It was not used as a substitute for the teacher but as an extra resource that the teacher could deploy. This raises the question of which is the learning affordance here: whether the effect came from more effective tutoring, or from having an extra aid (that might not be as effective but still an extra) to the teacher?

ACKNOWLEDGING THE LEARNER'S FEELINGS

Much of the early work on AI as a tutor treated learners as if they were disembodied learning mechanisms rather than human beings. Of course, they might offer words of praise if the learner correctly answered a question, but there was no particular reasoning about the individual learner to assess what kind of feedback was most appropriate or how it should be expressed.

Assessing and reasoning about learners' feelings and motivation have received a lot of attention over the last decade or so. Various methods have been developed to assess learners' feelings including videoing their faces and looking for smiles and frowns, looking at their body posture to see if they are leaning in or out in relation to the screen, wiring them up to look at their pulses or skin resistance, asking the learners to report how they feel or inferring feelings from the learner's behaviour. By trying to identify how a learner is feeling or how motivated they are, the teaching system can then adjust its feedback and its choice of next task accordingly. Wayang Outpost is an example of this approach for teaching school mathematics [8].

Wayang Outpost kept track of how many errors each learner made, how many hints they requested and how much time they were taking in answering questions to classify learners into different personas. These personas included those who seemed to achieve mastery without much effort, those who achieved mastery with high effort, those who abused the hint facility and did not evidence much effort, those who engaged in quick guessing without much effort, those who had worked hard but not achieved mastery, among several other persona types. For each persona, the system would have a rule about the next problem for that student, namely either harder, easier or about the same difficulty. It also had rules about affective and motivational feedback, e.g. praising effort, de-emphasising the importance of immediate success and showing learning progress so far. So, for example, a competent student who had achieved mastery without much effort would be offered more difficult problems and shown a chart of his or her good progress. In contrast, a student who had worked hard but not achieved mastery would have that effort acknowledged and praised and then be offered simpler problems next.

GETTING THE LEARNER TO THINK ABOUT LEARNING

Tutors not only teach stuff but also help students learn how to learn. We have already seen an instance of this in Chapter 2, where the pedagogical agent, teacher Mr Davis in the system Betty's Brain, would comment to the human student about the way they were going about learning ecology. Meta-Tutor is a system that has specialised in helping students improve their self-regulated learning capability. This is a skill that needs to be learned in particular contexts, and the context for Meta-Tutor is "*human body systems such as the circulatory, digestive, and nervous systems*" [9]. This system aims to help learners to set learning goals and also:

> models, prompts, and supports a learners' self-regulatory processes (to some degree) which may include cognitive (e.g., activating prior knowledge planning, creating sub-goals, learning strategies), metacognitive (e.g., feeling of knowing, judgment of learning, evaluate emerging understanding), motivational (e.g., self-efficacy, task value, interest, effort), affective (e.g., frustration, surprise, delight), or behavior (e.g., engaging in help-seeking behavior, modifying learning conditions; handling task difficulties and demands). [9, page 15]

The above is a good agenda for a human teacher too.

EVALUATING TUTORING SYSTEMS USING OUR FRAMEWORK

STEP 1: WHAT WE ARE GOOD AT, WHAT ARE MACHINES GOOD AT?

Human teachers are (in principle) good at knowing their students, what motivates them and what worries them and finding ways either to get them interested in whatever it is that needs to be learned or to unblock whatever it is that is impeding their learning [10]. When the teachers have the time, they are also good at providing detailed help with a learner's problem-solving or conceptual misunderstanding. This contextualising skill is what human tutors are very good at, in contrast to AI-based tutors which are good at generalising.

In contrast, machines are less versatile, but they are good at providing detailed help with a learner's problem-solving. In particular, they are less good in terms of knowing their students, despite access to their keystrokes, because who the learners are is not really defined by their keystrokes.

As we have shown above, progress is being made along a number of dimensions of teaching including recognising that learners have feelings, but we are a long way from being able to computationally duplicate the social and contextual aspects of teaching.

STEP 2: HOW CAN HUMANS AND MACHINES WORK TOGETHER?

In many classrooms, the two scarce resources are the teacher's time and the learners' wish to learn. So a good way for human teachers and machines to work together is for the human teacher to enthuse the learners, to sort them out when they get into muddles or are despondent. For their part, the machines are endlessly patient and can observe, comment and provide guidance either to individual learners or to groups of learners. Of course, the human teacher needs to be around when the learners' interactions with the machines break down or reach an impasse. The human teacher is also in a much better position to guide the learners through some reflective activity about what they have done, undertook and achieved. We propose that machines can make effective teaching assistants under the overall management of the human teacher. In terms of the paradigms for the division of labour between humans and AI, described in Chapter 1, we view this use of AI as a teaching assistant as a 'Human–AI Transactive collaboration', each with their own clear roles.

STEP 3: WHAT ARE THE CHARACTERISTICS OF AN EFFECTIVE TEACHER?

As indicated above, an effective teacher understands the overall social context within which they are teaching as well as the hopes, expectations, strengths and weaknesses of the learners. Whether teaching a tricky skill or a complex concept, the good teacher will be sensitive to how the learning process feels like for the learner and of the possible missteps, misunderstandings and awkwardness that naturally accompany learning something difficult.

In terms of the TACT framework of affordances and constraints described in Chapter 1, the very humanity of the human teacher is definitely an affordance in the highly social act of tutoring, and a definite constraint and limitation for AI. This further underlines the division of labour mentioned in Step 2, because the AI system really cannot do some parts of the tutoring job that only a human tutor can manage.

STEP 4: HOW CAN THIS AI TECHNOLOGY BE INTEGRATED INTO THE CLASSROOM?

Educational technology in general, and AI technology in particular, can be integrated into the classroom if it works reliably and can be set up, managed and fixed by technical staff. A second requirement is that the educational ethos of the technology is a good fit to that of the human teacher and the human teacher understands broadly how the technology works, what it is good at and bad at, where it is likely to confuse the learners and how its shortcomings can be circumvented.

Just because a piece of AI technology was designed to work one-to-one with a learner does not mean that is the only way to use it. Getting learners to work in small groups with such systems can often be as effective as solo work. There are two issues here. First is that a great deal of learning has a collaborative aspect in that coming to understand a concept or master a skill is achieved through dialogue. The act of trying to voice (or write) what one cannot yet quite understand and get some response aids learning. Second, such dialogues often take place in the context of tutoring where the other party to the learner is the tutor. But the other party can also be another learner. This relates back to the pedagogical knowledge introduced in the discussion of TPAC(D)K in Chapter 1. One aspect of pedagogical expertise is precisely to have a good sense of how to best exploit all of the resources within an educational context, especially the other learners.

STEP 5: REFLECT AND ITERATE

We have described above several Artificial Intelligent tutors as if they were finished products, complete in themselves. All of the systems we have described have undergone a large number of experimental evaluations in real classrooms and have been developed over time. Very often such systems have been modelled on expert human teachers as they provide the gold standard.

REFERENCES

1. De Grave, W. S., Dolmans, D. H. J. M., & Van Der Vleuten, C. P. M. (1999). Profiles of effective tutors in problem-based learning: Scaffolding student learning. *Medical Education*, 33(12), 901–906. doi:10.1046/j.1365-2923. 1999.00492.x

2. Carbonell, J. R. (1970). AI in CAI: An Artificial-Intelligence approach to computer-assisted instruction. *IEEE Transactions On Man-Machine Systems, MMS*, 11(4), 190–202.

3. Johnson, W. L. (2019). Data-driven development and evaluation of enskill English. *International Journal of Artificial Intelligence in Education*, 29(3), 425–457. doi:10.1007/s40593-019-00182-2

4. Biswas, G., Segedy, J. R., & Bunchongchit, K. (2016). From design to implementation to practice a learning by teaching system: Betty's Brain. *International Journal of Artificial Intelligence in Education*, 26(1), 350–364. doi:10.1007/s40593-015-0057-9

5. Dweck, C. S. (2017). *Mindset: Changing the way you think to fulfil you potential*. London, UK: Robinson.

6. Karam, R., Pane, J. F., Griffin, B. A., Robyn, A., Phillips, A., & Daugherty, L. (2017). Examining the implementation of technology-based blended algebra I curriculum at scale. *Educational Technology Research & Development*, 65, 399–425. doi:10.1007/s11423-016-9498-6

7. Pane, J. F., Griffin, B. A., McCaffrey, D. F., & Karam, R. (2014). Effectiveness of cognitive tutor Algebra I at scale. *Educational Evaluation and Policy Analysis*, 36(2), 127–144. doi:10.3102/0162373713507480

8. Arroyo, I., Woolf, B. P., Burleson, W., Muldner, K., Rai, D., & Tai, M. (2014). A multimedia adaptive tutoring system for mathematics that addresses cognition, metacognition and affect. *International Journal of Artificial Intelligence in Education*, 24(4), 387–426.

9. Azevedo, R., Witherspoon, A., Chauncey, A., Burkett, C., & Fike, A. (2009). MetaTutor: A metacognitive tool for enhancing self-regulated learning. Paper presented at the AAAI Fall Symposium (FS-09-02).

10. Rosiek, J. (2003). Emotional scaffolding: An exploration of the teacher knowledge at the intersection of student emotion and the subject matter. *Journal of Teacher Education*, 54(4), 399–412.

4

AI AS A CLASSROOM MODERATOR

HOW CAN AI GIVE ME EYES IN THE BACK OF MY HEAD?

Figure 4.1 How can AI give me eyes in the back of my head? Illustrated by Yael Toiber Kent.

DOI: 10.1201/9781003194545-4

Synopsis: This chapter explains how a teacher can use AI to keep tabs on everyone in her class so she can choose who to go and help first.

It discusses how artificial intelligence can relieve some of the burden of classroom management from teachers and enable them to concentrate more on the motivational, emotional and cognitive aspects of teaching.

BACKGROUND

Whether virtual or not, a classroom is a most complex system. At a given time, in a single room, there would usually be two or more dozen students, whose differences would outnumber their similarities. Each of them would be bringing into the classroom a full personal ecosystem of motivational, emotional, social and cognitive factors; memories of where they are coming from; and the anticipation towards where they will be going to when they leave the classroom. A complex network of interactions would be spread among the classroom's participants, the taught subjects, the texts, images, maps, videos, concepts and arguments with which they would be interacting in the next few hours. Noise, lighting, relationships, instructions, demands, questions, mind-wandering, doors, windows, books, attention spans, computers and software agents all exist and operate simultaneously in a strongly connected, sensory overloaded and unpredictable sequence of events (see Figure 4.2).

And usually just one teacher, with one pair of ears, one pair of eyes, some sort of familiarity with the learners, and some sort of understanding of what they each do, understand and learn at any given minute. For the teacher to be doing their job, namely, to teach and support different learners in various ways, and provide feedback, this whole chaotic orchestra must first − be reasonably managed.

<u>Classroom orchestration</u> refers to the management of classroom work, involving small group, individual and whole-class activities [1, 2], usually by a single 'conductor' − the teacher who, in addition

to (and even before) teaching, is also responsible for making "*timely and context-relevant adjustments to the script based on assessments of individual and whole class progress, collaboration and growth of ideas*" [3].

Using technology to support teachers in classroom management or orchestration is a well-researched and investigated area [4]. Clearly, classrooms were managed way before orchestration technologies were available. However, some seemingly unrelated trends led to a rising need to support teachers in their orchestration.

First, the introduction of technology (tutoring systems in particular) in schools put the students behind screens, which, on the one hand, shifted the teachers' focus from teaching and tutoring to assuming mediating roles. On the other hand, the students' independent mode of work enabled by tutoring systems made it harder for teachers to have a decent understanding of what their students were doing and where they were struggling. In a wider context, technology enables remote learning, such as in blended and online learning. Teaching remotely means the teachers can no longer rely on their physical presence, and on their own eyes and ears, to monitor and manage the classroom.

Second, over the last decade, pedagogical views on instruction have shifted. Instead of an instructional approach that is based on teachers 'transferring' knowledge and students passively absorbing it, teachers are now encouraged to implement a 'student-centred' approach. In this approach, knowledge is seen as co-constructed by both the teacher and the students rather than transmitted directly by the teacher. Classrooms are seen as 'learning communities' and the focus of the classroom activity planning turned to inquiry-based learning, active learning and social construction of knowledge [5]. Implementing pedagogies that require high involvement of the students can no longer be achieved in the totally compliant, 19th-century-like classrooms. In fact, the more the emphasis is placed on student choice, agency and mobility, the more unpredictable the learning environment becomes, thus leading to a need for more resources for classroom monitoring and management.

Third, skills in some subjects, e.g. STEM subjects, and teachers who are teaching outside their subject expertise are in shortage. Classrooms managed by supply teachers, teaching assistants or less qualified or experienced teachers require more support in orchestration activities.

What role can artificial intelligence play in supporting teachers in classroom moderation and orchestration? For example, based on prior data about students, AI could support teachers assigning them to appropriate groups. The use of AI in computer systems could help learners improve coordination within the groups by adding 'noise' (acting randomly or in a meaningless way) to their work [6]. Perhaps most importantly, AI could serve as an effective additional set of eyes and ears for the teacher. By collecting evidence and data, AI could enhance teachers' awareness by enabling them to track students' progress in real time, adjust the time required by different students and groups according to their needs and direct the teachers' attention to critical moments in their students' learning [7].

Holstein et al. [8] found that when teachers are given the choice, they would choose to use AI in real time to identify and assess students who most need assistance and to then evaluate the impacts of that assistance. Students, on the other hand, preferred to utilise AI to let their teachers know that they need help without losing face to peers. However, they still wished to receive emotional support from human teachers, rather than from AI. According to Holstein et al. [9], using AI in orchestrating the classroom led to a fairer allocation of the teacher's time in class (as teachers used their time helping students who actually needed help, as opposed to those seeking support most loudly). They also found that the effect of the orchestration system on students knowing they are being monitored resulted in less 'hint abuse' (i.e. trying to get the computer to answer the question or solve the problem), 'hint avoidance' (i.e. failing to make use of the help that was available from the computer) and 'gaming the system' (i.e. finding ways to appear to be succeeding when in fact they were not).

In addition to teaching challenges that relate to the cognitive aspects of the classroom, orchestration can also focus on the operational aspect of classroom flow, taking place before, during and after the lesson.

Before the lesson, AI systems can support the design and planning of the lesson. This would typically include preparing materials, pedagogical strategies, tasks and groupings, while accommodating the various needs and abilities of the different students. **During class**, the primary challenges which teachers face relate to classroom management in real time. These include the coordination of the lesson's flow, while synchronising the planned design with the actual turn of events and interactions taking place in the classroom. It is vital for the teacher to be able to adjust to (sometimes unexpected) changes in the flow of the lesson and to design interventions on the spot in case there is a need. **After the class** (and sometimes during), formative and summative assessments might take place for both individuals or groups and the class as a whole. While **during** the class, AI would focus on enhancing teachers' awareness of the class dynamics and real-time support mechanisms, the focus **after** the class would typically be on providing feedback and evaluating students' progress [10, 11].

EXAMPLES OF ORCHESTRATION SYSTEMS

In the context of classroom orchestration, we can look at the orchestrating system vs. the orchestrated system [12], the latter being the outcome of the former. Obviously, neither has to be a technological (or AI in particular) system. An orchestrating system could be the teachers, along with their lesson plans and sets of tools and practices. A technological orchestrating system would work to augment or support the teacher in managing curricular activities [13]. For example, the Texas Instruments Nspire Navigator enables the teacher to control the flow of the class through actions such as projecting a student's screen to the front of the class for all to see or sending quizzes to the students to assess their progress [14].

Orchestrated systems are the systems whose precise function can be determined or adapted by the orchestrating system. An orchestrated system could be as simple as the lesson as planned and carried out by the teacher, remote access into the students' screens or a cognitive tutoring system that enables students to progress at their own pace [7].

For example, Holstein [9] designed a set of mixed-reality 'smart glasses' (i.e. spectacles that show the real world with some computer-generated text or images superimposed) that direct teachers' attention in real time (the orchestrating system) based on data collected about the students' progress with individual access to a tutoring system (the orchestrated system). The researchers were able to show that the combination of the orchestrating with the orchestrated systems enhanced student learning, compared with a tutoring system-only classroom, where the orchestrating was done by the teacher alone. Mavrikis et al. [15] designed a suite of visualisation and notification tools, with the aim of assisting teachers in focusing their attention effectively while students were working with an algebra tutoring system. Using a non-real-time orchestrating mechanism, Merceron and Yacef [16] collected data from a tutoring tool used at the University of Sydney, to cluster the student answers, based on the mistakes they made using the tutoring tool. The aim of the clustering was to assist the teacher in getting a sense of the prevalent mistakes made by various groups of students. Finally, Cheema et al. [17] report on a paper-based classroom system called Classroom Challenges (CCs). Teachers orchestrating the work with CC themselves experienced a high workload, since they had to analyse the students' work and provide feedback almost on the spot. To assist the teachers, Cheema et al. developed an orchestrating technology called FACT. Operating on a tablet, FACT enabled the teacher to assign CC tasks, create groups, view the students' work, provide feedback and share it with the class.

THE ARCHITECTURE OF ORCHESTRATION SYSTEMS

Figure 4.2 illustrates the general architecture of an orchestrating eco-system in the classroom. In essence, most orchestrating systems are designed to augment the teachers' awareness and decision-making, which is assumed to lead to improved teaching, and consequently, to improved learning. At a very basic level, this would assume that students are engaging with classroom artefacts and the orchestrated system and that this engagement produces 'footprints' or a data trail (either digital or not). If some students are not engaging (or at least behaving in an observable way), footprints such as questions, answers, discussions, arguments, drawing, heartbeats, system logs or sensor logs are not being created and the teacher would need to

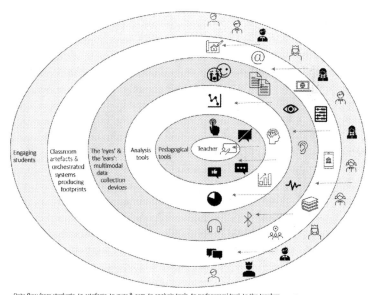

Data flow from students, to artefacts, to eyes & ears, to analysis tools, to pedagogical tool, to the teacher

Figure 4.2 An architecture of a classroom orchestrating ecosystem. Following the arrows, data flow from right to left: from students, to artefacts, to eyes and ears, to analysis tools, to pedagogical tool, to the teacher.

work with such students to try and rebuild their motivation. At the third level in the diagram, this architecture assumes that there are 'eyes and ears' (again either digital or not), consuming those raw footprints and collecting them. Further analysis would take place on the raw data (again, either via technology or a human brain) at the fourth level, making sure the teacher would receive meaningful, clear and actionable data. At the fifth level are the pedagogical tools available for the direct use of the teachers. As before, these may be either digital tools (such as clusters of students, notifications and recommendations) or human tools (such as human-led interventions and feedback).

The last decade has brought significant growth in the use of sensors and other automatic data-collection methods, which could be considered as 'eyes and ears'. In addition to becoming mainstream in everyday use (such as the Internet of Things for 'smart homes' and wearables for healthcare tracking) these are also used in educational settings. For example, electroencephalogram (EEG) monitoring electric activity in the brain has been used for detecting cognitive skills that affect learning, such as focused attention and the use of working memory [18], or PDA data by infrared tracking a student walking across the classroom [19].

ANALYSIS OF ORCHESTRATION SYSTEMS

Several frameworks have been developed for the analysis and pedagogical tool tiers (shown in Figure 4.2) in the last few years. For example, Martinez-Maldonado et al. [20] designed MTFeedback, whose main goal was to automatically provide teachers with **notifications about group learning** activities during a lesson. Chen [21] presented a system for monitoring messages sent between students working in a group and offering teachers information such as a summary of activity and focused recommendations for direct teacher actions. Dillenbourg et al. [13] created a system presenting information on a large display to support reflection on group activities and to help the teacher follow the progress achieved within groups. Kent and Cukurova [22] suggested a set of metrics for evaluating the collaboration process in online learning discussions in order to help the teacher assess the quality of collaborative learning. Casamayor [23] designed a system monitoring students' participation in an online learning environment, which notified teachers when **conflicts were detected**. Also, in the context of group work in class, AI has been utilised for **team formation** [24] or for **group moderation** [6]. Dynamic conversational support for collaborative learning has been designed to provide automated **feedback regarding how well students perform their roles in the groups**, with the aim of helping them assist each other [25].

Yacef [26] developed a system enabling computer science teachers to monitor the in-class and after-class progress and to **identify frequent mistakes**. Mazza and Dimitrova [27] designed a set of metrics showing the teacher the **general progress and engagement levels** of students in online learning. Dillenbourg [13] developed a gadget that students could use to **seek feedback from the teachers and indicate their progress**. Rojas et al. [28] also designed a monitoring tool that a teacher could carry during a lab session. The tool indicated to the teacher when **particular students had requested feedback** and **which students had already been attended to**. Tissenbaum and Slotta [7] developed a tablet application that allowed the teacher to get a full picture of the classroom in real time, to help them identify **when and where they were needed**.

EVALUATING ORCHESTRATING SYSTEMS

In this section, we explore general issues around orchestration by applying our five-step evaluation framework to a fictional orchestrating system. In this fictional scenario we look at the issues through the eyes of Edtech designers, interested in developing a teacher awareness augmentation system, similar to many examples we have mentioned in this chapter. We would look into supporting secondary-school teachers who might wish to use this fictional system to implement social learning more effectively, using AI. Being hit by a global pandemic, their school has now decided to put in place the infrastructure needed to support remote learning, while also keeping the students engaged and learning socially.

From the point of view of the Edtech designers, their early adoptors will be teachers who have indicated an interest in using collaborative learning both synchronously (using video calls and group chats), as well as asynchronously, using online discussions platforms, to discuss specific topics, to research collaboratively and to debate. Teaching remotely and not being able to monitor closely what is going on in their classrooms, the teachers indicated that they wanted to get useful learning analytics to understand whether their students are collaborating effectively, and to be able to respond if they were not.

This would be a classic 'eyes and ears' scenario, which needs to also connect to some provision of pedagogical support for the teachers. The teachers in our fictional scenario did not want the system to communicate directly with the students, as they chose to keep the direct support component for themselves. Specifically, the teachers wished to use: (1) daily summaries on the level of engagement and participation of the whole class, as well as of individual students, in both synchronous and asynchronous discussions; and (2) daily alerts on significant changes to an individual student's or to the whole class's engagement, which might require their further investigation, adjustment to the instructional design or individual intervention. Such alerts might indicate a change in the overall class collaborative performance (for example, the class as a community is showing a decline in their mutual sharing patterns or a specific group of students are being 'left out' of the discussion). In this case, our fictional teachers would be able to explore what kinds of adaptations to the lesson plan are needed to get the class interacting effectively again. In addition, the alerts might indicate significant individual changes, identifying groups of students with specific interaction patterns, or providing early signs for disengagement.

STEP 1: MAP OUT OUR/THEIR UNFAIR ADVANTAGES

First, we must determine which skills and abilities will most effectively be attributed to teachers vs. those which will best belong to the system. In contrast to other AI education systems, orchestration systems tend to be less concerned with subject domain knowledge or social features. The users of these systems would typically be teachers. In this combination of teachers and machines working together, the humans' unfair advantage would be their ability to connect and support the students motivationally, socially and emotionally (employing social intelligence), their ability to improvise when a change in the lesson plan is required, and their meta-subjective intelligence (which means the ability to recognise our own emotions and the emotions of others) [29]. In this scenario, the teacher would therefore be the only one interacting with the students and planning the lesson, as well as any potential changes and adaptations. Not less importantly, the teacher would be the only one responsible for the relevance of the curriculum and its pedagogy and for the quality of the content of the discussion.

The machines' significant advantages in this context are that they act potentially as <u>multimodal</u> 'eyes and ears' for teachers, that is, able to collect data generated by different sources and types. AI software is good at interacting with various types of hardware (such as visual, auditory and touch sensors), at integrating data produced from various resources, at processing huge amounts of these data on the fly and at eliminating noise in this data. However, should we be concerned about this practically limitless ability of technology to 'hear' and 'see'?

Timms [30] envisioned 'Educational Cobots' to be robots working alongside human teachers. The cobot has the unfair advantage of being able to move around the classroom (physical as well as virtual, although Timms was referring to physical classrooms in this instance). As students are working in the class, the cobot is able to track a student leaving the classroom without permission (using high-definition cameras, motion sensors or biometric sensors like wristbands devices), recognising facial expression (using facial recognition technologies) and vocal tones of students, and tracking blood volume pulse and galvanic skin response to detect the students' mood and focus. *"It's easy for a teacher to spot if a group is noisier than the rest of the room, but not to detect if the level of discussion dropped because they are not talking to each other in a collaborative task for example"* [30]. Referring to an earlier example, Roschelle and Pea [19] described tracking students' movements across the classroom to make it 'publicly visible and tangible' to the teacher and other students. However, an important question to be asked is − **just because we could have 'eyes' and 'ears' all over the classroom, should we?** Does the teacher really need to monitor every move, rise in blood pressure due to excitement or stress, and every change in tone and smile in order to orchestrate the class? What about the students' sense of privacy and self-consciousness (especially among young people) and their right to not be so exposed? And if we think it is a good idea, how long should that data be kept and who else but the teacher should be able to see it?

STEP 2: CHOOSING A COLLABORATION PARADIGM

Within orchestration systems, there is a need to find a delicate balance between automation and teacher autonomy. At the outset, using AI in orchestration was a way to relieve teachers' burden. However, classroom moderation and orchestration both require an element of human interaction and flexibility with the lesson planning that could be hindered with the use of the 'thinking machines' or the 'intelligent extensions' collaboration paradigms (see Figure 1.3 in Chapter 1). How do we determine the right balance? Is the human teacher merely a 'part of the loop' or the other way around; i.e. will the AI be a part of a human-dominated orchestration loop? Are we envisioning a synergy between artificial intelligence and human teachers or distinct roles for each?

To figure out which collaboration paradigm we should use to build our fictional system, we asked ourselves some of the questions mentioned in Chapter 1. For instance, we had no doubt about the accountability for the decisions made. We were going to leave it up to our teachers to decide whether and how to adjust classroom flows, even though the system's inputs would have informed their choices. Clearly, the data-collection tasks would be handled by the AI. Teachers will be presented with a set processed metrics and alerts, and they will translate these into pedagogical decisions. We would have felt confident with leaving the agency and accountability in the hands of teachers, as the AI was not designed to engage directly with students, nor would it have the wisdom to know what to do with that data. In any case, the AI's role was very prescribed and far from making (or even implementing) decisions. Then again, in order to implement the 'transactive collaboration approach', where the machine would join a human loop instead of the other way around, the teachers would have to engage in a design process of the metrics and alerts used. Having the teachers themselves designing those metrics (rather than just 'having a say') would help the AI play its role in a meaningful way, which in turn would serve the teachers' pedagogical views. It would also make it easier for the teachers to hold full accountability for the orchestration action.

STEP 3: WHAT WOULD AN EFFECTIVE ORCHESTRATION SYSTEM AFFORD ITS USERS?

Now that we have identified what roles the human and the AI are best positioned to take, and how to integrate them, the next step would be to identify the learning affordances and limitations of such a collaboration for teachers. To remind ourselves, a learning affordance is defined (in our case) as a feature that the teacher can both perceive and act upon to achieve a desired result of interacting with our system. The limitations (or constraints) are those that teachers might perceive as imposing on them or preventing them from achieving the goals of orchestrating their classroom effectively. The main assumption behind the design of our fictitious orchestration system is that the AI system would enhance the teachers' awareness, and take over some of their current burden to monitor their students' collaborative work. This in turn would potentially improve their teaching, for example, by freeing their time to be spent on one-on-one teaching, or by simply becoming more aware of their students' collaborative behaviour. Having more effective teaching is expected, in turn, to improve their students' learning.

What would the system need to enable for that to happen? For instance, whatever the orchestrated technology is (e.g. forum discussions, small groups collaborative documents or video calls), there is a need for the orchestrating system to be able to collect and analyse the interactional data they produce in an efficient way (hence, to be the teachers multiple 'eyes and ears'). This means collecting data from multiple data sources, applicable to various tasks and topics, from the multiple physical locations of the students' working stations, throughout multiple points in time. Looking at potential limitations, transmitting this data in **a non-secure way** would be a huge limitation imposed by our system. For example, even if the data does stream in a very timely and efficient way, but exposes the personal footprints of the students to third party applications or people, then these efficient eyes and ears might become more damaging than enabling.

Another main affordance of the system would be to make the processed information **accessible to the teachers in a clear, timely and actionable way, and in a way that would not restrict the students' ability to express themselves.** For example, Martinez-Maldonado et al. [31] confirmed in their orchestration system design that the data presented to the teachers was able to drive their focus of attention and that the teachers valued their group work and individual participation's indicators of group work. A potential limitation might be that the information provided to the teachers would be distracting, unclear or simply drive the focus of attention off the students altogether, or off those students who mostly need their support.

We now consider any potential limitations to the flow of classroom activities. Clearly, our fictional system should first and foremost not cause any loss of learning opportunities. Dillenbourg et al. [13] discussed ways in which an orchestrating system could hinder the classroom flow by imposing 'rigidness' or inability to adapt. For example, they mention events such as a student dropping out from a group at the last minute, a last-minute change in the defined task or students refusing to work together as examples in which AI systems might not adapt to very well. These cases demonstrate exactly how AI would fall short when things are not going as expected, which is in fact – an everyday reality in classrooms.

STEP 4: EVALUATING THE IMPACT OF THE AI SYSTEM IN THE CLASSROOM

Once we evaluate the potential affordances and limitations of our system, we need to figure out whether it stands a chance of making it through the reality test of being successfully integrated into a classroom. In general, the adoption of learning analytics (e.g. collecting detailed learner data) within schools is still slow. Even more so is the integration of meaningful learning analytics that could reveal patterns of collaborative learning [22]. As mentioned earlier, to ensure successful adoption, it is crucial to follow our secondary-school teachers' views, practices and challenges very carefully [32]. As an example of how to design a technology-based instructional strategy using TPAC(D)K, we use the context of a fictitious sociology class in a secondary school.

The content knowledge (CK) includes topics such as education and crime. The pedagogical knowledge uses online discussions to accomplish two main goals. First, to allow physically distanced students (due to school closure, for example) to study remotely as a group, learn to collaborate and discuss respectfully, and build their arguments on top of those of their peers. The second objective is to have the students practice critical thinking and to establish evidence-based arguments among the students, by allowing them to debate important sociological issues. The technological knowledge (TK) is in terms of using an online discussion platform which allows the students to connect their newly created posts to their peers' already existing posts, while also allowing them to express the relationship they see between their own and their peers' posts. Utilising our orchestration system, the data knowledge (DK) is used to present data about the class and about individual students to the teacher. At the collective level, the teacher is able to determine how inclusive and interactive the group is. At the individual student's level, the system would show the teacher indicators of how active and interactive the students are on any given day, how much attention they put into their dialogue and on building their arguments on top of others' (rather than building it based on their own views alone).

STEP 5: COLLECT EVIDENCE, REFLECT AND ITERATE

We mentioned earlier that our main assumption behind the design of our fictitious orchestration system was that the artificial intelligence system would enhance teachers' awareness as well as relieve some of their burden by monitoring students' collaborative work. Then we assumed that this unburdening and awareness augmentation would improve the teaching, for instance, by making the teachers spend more time on one-to-one instruction or by making teachers more aware of their students' collaborative behaviours. Having more effective teaching was expected – in turn – to improve the students' learning. But how do we know whether our assumptions will be realised? The fifth step of the framework is all about gathering evidence from the class integration intervention that was described in Step 4, reflecting on it and attempting to modify our assumptions and design choices, then iterate and evaluate again.

REFERENCES

1. Dillenbourg, P. (2013). Design for classroom orchestration. *Computers & Education*, 69, 485–492.
2. Roschelle, J., Dimitriadis, Y., & Hoppe, U. (2013). Classroom orchestration: Synthesis. *Computers & Education*, 69, 523–526.

3. Sharples, M. (2013). Shared orchestration within and beyond the classroom. *Computers & Education*, 69(1), 504–506. doi:10.1016/j.compedu.2013.04.014

4. Tissenbaum, M., Matuk, C., Berland, M., Lyons, L., Cocco, F., Linn, M., …, Dillenbourg, P. (2016). Real-time visualization of student activities to support classroom orchestration. In ICLS 2016 (pp. 1120–1127).

5. Garrett, T. (2008). Student-centered and teacher-centered classroom management: A case study of three elementary teachers. *The Journal of Classroom Interaction*, 43, 34–47.

6. Shirado, H., & Christakis, N. A. (2017). Locally noisy autonomous agents improve global human coordination in network experiments. *Nature*, 545(7654), 370–374.

7. Tissenbaum, M., & Slotta, J. (2019). Supporting classroom orchestration with real-time feedback: A role for teacher dashboards and real-time agents. *International Journal of Computer-Supported Collaborative Learning*, 14(3), 325–351.

8. Holstein, K., McLaren, B. M., & Aleven, V. (2019, June). Designing for complementarity: Teacher and student needs for orchestration support in AI-enhanced classrooms. In *International conference on Artificial Intelligence in education* (pp. 157–171). Springer, Cham.

9. Holstein, K., McLaren, B.M., Aleven, V. (2018). Student learning benefits of a mixed-reality teacher awareness tool in AI-enhanced classrooms. In *International conference on Artificial Intelligence in education* (pp. 154–168). Springer (2018).

10. Martinez-Maldonado, R., Schneider, B., Charleer, S., Shum, S. B., Klerkx, J., & Duval, E. (2016, April). Interactive surfaces and learning analytics: Data, orchestration aspects, pedagogical uses and challenges. In *Proceedings of the Sixth international conference on learning analytics & knowledge* (pp. 124–133).

11. Prieto, L. P., Dlab, M. H., Gutiérrez, I., Abdulwahed, M., & Balid, W. (2011). Orchestrating technology enhanced learning: A literature review and a conceptual framework. *International Journal of Technology Enhanced Learning*, 3(6), 583–598. doi:10.1504/ijtel.2011.045449

12. Tchounikine, P. (2013). Clarifying design for orchestration: Orchestration and orchestrable technology, scripting and conducting. *Computers & Education*, 69, 500–503. doi:10.1016/j.compedu.2013.04.006

13. Dillenbourg, P., Zufferey, G., Alavi, H., Jermann, P., Do-Lenh, S., Bonnard, Q., … & Kaplan, F. (2011). Classroom orchestration: The third circle of

usability. In *proceedings of the International conference on Computer Supported Learning* (CSCL2011) (pp. 510–517).

14. Clark-Wilson, A. (2010). Emergent pedagogies and the changing role of the teacher in the TI-Nspire navigator- networked mathematics classroom. *ZDM*, 42(7), 747–761.

15. Mavrikis, M., Gutierrez-Santos, S., & Poulovassilis, A. (2016, April). Design and evaluation of teacher assistance tools for exploratory learning environments. In *Proceedings of the sixth international conference on learning analytics & knowledge* (pp. 168–172).

16. Merceron, A., & Yacef, K. (2004, August). Clustering students to help evaluate learning. In *IFIP World Computer Congress,TC 3* (pp. 31–42). Springer, Boston, MA.

17. Cheema, S., VanLehn, K., Burkhardt, H., Pead, D., & Schoenfeld, A. (2016). Electronic posters to support formative assessment. In Proceedings of the 2016 CHI *conference extended abstracts on human factors in computing systems* (pp. 1159–1164).

18. Mohamed, Z., El Halaby, M., Said, T., Shawky, D., & Badawi, A. (2019). Facilitating classroom orchestration using EEG to detect the cognitive states of learners. In *International conference on advanced machine learning technologies and applications* (pp. 209–217). Springer, Cham.

19. Roschelle, J. & Pea, R. (2002). A walk on the WILD side: How wireless handhelds may change computer-supported collaborative learning. *International Journal of Cognition and Technology*, 1(2), 145–168.

20. Martinez-Maldonado, R., Clayphan, A., Yacef, K., & Kay, J. (2014). MTFeedback: providing notifications to enhance teacher awareness of small group work in the classroom. *IEEE Transactions on Learning Technologies*, 8(2), 187–200.

21. Chen, W. (2004). Supporting teachers intervention in collaborative knowledge building. *Journal of Network and Computer Applications*, 9, 200–215.

22. Kent, C., & Cukurova, M. (2020). Investigating collaboration as a process with theory-driven learning analytics. *Journal of Learning Analytics*, 7(1), 59–71.

23. Casamayor, A., Amandi, A., & Campo, M. (2009). Intelligent assistance for teachers in collaborative e-learning environments. *Computers & Education*, 53(4), 1147–1154.

24. Alberola, J. M., Del Val, E., Sanchez-Anguix, V., Palomares, A., & Teruel, M. D. (2016). An artificial intelligence tool for heterogeneous team formation in the classroom. *Knowledge-Based Systems*, 101, 1–14.

25. Sankaranarayanan, S., Kandimalla, S. R., Hasan, S., An, H., Bogart, C., Murray, R. C., ... & Rosé, C. (2020, July). Agent-in-the-loop: Conversational agent support in service of reflection for learning during collaborative programming. In *International conference on Artificial Intelligence in education* (pp. 273–278). Springer, Cham.

26. Yacef, K. (2005). The logic-ITA in the classroom: A medium scale experiment. *International Journal of Artificial Intelligence in Education*, 15(1), 41–62.

27. Mazza, R., & Dimitrova, V. (2004), Visualising student tracking data to support instructors in web-based distance education. In *Proc. Int. World Wide Web Conf.* Alternate Track Papers Posters, 2004 (pp. 154–161).

28. Rojas, I. G., García, R. M. C., & Kloos, C. D. (2012). Enhancing orchestration of lab sessions by means of awareness mechanisms. In *European Conference on technology enhanced learning* (pp. 113–125). Springer, Berlin, Heidelberg.

29. Luckin, R. (2018). *Machine learning and Human Intelligence: The future of education for the 21st century.* UCL IOE Press. London, UK.

30. Timms, M. J. (2016). Letting artificial intelligence in education out of the box: educational cobots and smart classrooms. *International Journal of Artificial Intelligence in Education*, 26(2), 701–712.

31. Martinez-Maldonado, R., Kay, J., Yacef, K., Edbauer, M. T., & Dimitriadis, Y. (2013). MTClassroom and MTDashboard: Supporting analysis of teacher attention in an orchestrated multi-tabletop classroom.

32. Prieto, L. P., Rodríguez-Triana, M. J., Martínez-Maldonado, R., Dimitriadis, Y., & Gašević, D. (2019). Orchestrating learning analytics (OrLA): Supporting inter-stakeholder communication about adoption of learning analytics at the classroom level. *Australasian Journal of Educational Technology*, 35(4), 14–33.

5

CONCLUSION

SO, ARE WE FRIENDS NOW?

Figure 5.1 So, are we friends now? Illustrated by Yael Toiber Kent.

DOI: 10.1201/9781003194545-5

Synopsis: This chapter concludes this book. It reflects on how AI could be used alongside teachers and learners, instead of against them – contributing to exclusion, threat, confusion or bias. When humanely designed, it could be also humanely used. Just like thinking or acting humanely, designing humanely means being considerate, thorough and respectful, which is what must lie at the heart of designing educational technology, and AI in particular. We, as users, designers, developers and decision-makers, need to remember that using AI does not reduce us to its level. Human beings will always be more intelligent, and with that comes accountability and responsibility.

My milk is definitely too hot … perhaps forty seconds in the microwave might be a bit too long". I am thinking – sharing with my Nix42 *Virtual Assistant* bot. "It certainly raised your body temperature, so you might be right", my Nix42 replies and offers – "Bella, do you think you'll be ready to start schooling in four minutes? By your biometrics, it looks as if you are ready". "Give me 10 minutes and I'll be ready", I reply. It's 5:12PM, my older brother had finished school for the day just a few minutes ago (as his 'biological clock' would suggest), and I'll be ready to begin my school day soon. Ten minutes later, I pass Kate in the virtual corridor of our school. Kate is one of my learning group mates. She lives on the other side of the globe, and she does not speak English, but our virtual assistants are able to make our chat complete with smart translation in real time, so I rarely think of her as coming from some far away place. When Kate and I get together, we sometimes share our learning data with each other. With the use of our secure learning records system connected to my Nix42, my parents and I control who gets which type of access to my personal learning data. Talking to Kate about things I have learnt, how it made me feel, and what makes me behave the way I do, helps me to understand myself better.

Mrs Tunningham, our teacher, supports us during the day in virtual labs where we are able to run several experiments in parallel, analyse data, and discuss the results while improving some important skills, such as problem-solving and critical thinking skills, with our classmates. Mrs Tunningham's virtual assistant ensures she always knows where and when each of us needs some support or attention. She is always telling us which 'piece of evidence' (as she calls it) made her realise what kind of support was effective (or ineffective) for us, so that she knows how to best help us next. Mrs Tunningham is usually available for any questions I have in between lessons, since most of the administration and assessment tasks are taken care of by bots. Although I know she does not always know all the facts in my textbook, I trust her to help me navigate my way forward and achieve my goals. When she is busy, my Nix42 offers me some useful feedback really quickly, such as when I do not support my argument with valid evidence, or when my group interaction was not as effective as it could have been, and why.

My Nix42 is also a great companion to my essay writing, and is helping me collect, evaluate, and integrate reliable sources of information to support my ideas. Adaptive digital textbooks are accompanying my progress in most of my lessons, and my Nix42 already knows me well enough to offer me some examples from subjects I am interested in (such as firefighting) to explain concepts I am struggling with (when studying physics, maths, English etc.).

Remember our Bella's reflection from this book's introduction? Remember how you felt about the prospects of AI being used wrongly in her daily routine? How does the reflection opening this chapter feel to you?

Just as the use of AI could be intrusive, discriminating and isolating, it could also be supportive, chatty and transparent. AI could be used to take the agency away from students, or it could be used to support students to develop their agency. It could be designed to replace teachers, or it could empower teachers to focus on those areas that AI could never do better anyway. AI could restrict young people's development, or it could open new opportunities and afford them personal and informed interactions with their surroundings.

At the end of the day, machines are not (and will not get) close to matching human intelligence. The trajectory of their cognition is completely different, and it is subject to our design choices.

We, humans, are the designers of our technologies, our pedagogical methods, our curriculums and the education of young people. We are accountable for their education, and it is up to us to decide whether their days at school will look closer to the prediction opening this book or to the one closing it.

AI systems do not carry a moral or conscience of their own. It is our morals that they are designed to follow, for better or worse. More often than not, they do a brilliant job at perpetuating the racism, discrimination and other biases that they detect in the societal patterns they were trained on. But it is our own societal failings that these algorithms are picking up and our own choice to use them.

For example, there have been online testing platforms that were trained on racially unbalanced populations and thus failing to identify students of colour [1] in high stakes exams (such as bar exams) or disadvantaging pupils of a lower socioeconomic background [2]. The crime of the designers of those systems was in trying to develop ways in which AI systems were 'accurate', without considering the wider picture. This meant – accurately mimicking (potentially flawed) human behaviour and logic. Instead of mimicking, perhaps we should aspire to design systems that seek to complement societal human faults.

The aspiration to bring AI as close as possible to human intelligence can sometimes yield absurd situations. For example, in evaluating AI decision-making, it is common to think of the fairness–accuracy trade-off. This means that typically, a 'fairer' system is less 'accurate', exactly because it is doing a lesser job in resembling human reality. And the human reality is rarely fair.

For example, an algorithm making an automatic decision to deny college admission to a person from a historically marginalised group might be doing so due to it being 'accurate'. That is, the decision is made on the basis of a long history of such wrong decisions. It might even be 'fair' in the sense that it treated this person in a 'blind' or 'unbiased' way. That is, equally to the way people from the dominant group are treated. But is that fair? In both those cases, the designers have preferred accuracy over historical fairness.

However, if the AI system recommends accepting this person's college application for the sake of correcting historical injustice, it might be considered as 'less accurate'.

If it was a human admissions' tutor making the same decision, their decision would not even be evaluated using the same 'accuracy' criteria as AI systems would be evaluated. AI is subjected to different evaluation criteria, stemming from our expectation that it should mimic past human decisions (which is rarely our expectation from humans).

Some researchers claim that there is no practical way to make data neutral (e.g. race-less or gender-less). In the United States, for example, merely deleting the data about someone's race would not suffice to mask it. Just looking at a person's ZIP code could give you a strong hint about their race. In that case, we would argue – the evaluation criteria should shift from fairness and accuracy to equity and from reducing harm to providing justice [3]. That is, evaluating a decision on the basis of giving people equal opportunities instead of trying to remain loyal to the accuracy of historical decisions or being fair (which is not a straightforward criterion anyway – fair to whom? To one marginalised group instead of another? To the majority?).

This raises another question – can we hold AI systems to moral principles that we do not hold ourselves to? If an educational system is built on a non-inclusive and discriminating infrastructure, can (or should) technology be making the first step towards shifting the power dynamics?

WE CERTAINLY COULD. BUT SHOULD WE?

In our work with educational companies and schools, we often speak with companies who are looking to explore innovative ways in which AI could be leveraged in their products. It is a strange era we live in: AI technologies are very affordable and doable, and we all feel this tickle of innovation runs through our fingertips. Because the technology is there, within our reach, and we can use it. But then again – we urge you to think – should we?

"All models are wrong, but some are useful" is a statement generally attributed to the statistician George Box. The main idea behind this statement is that statistical models (such as those that AI systems are based on) are essentially built on the principle of generalisation. The process of modelling (and statistics in general) is built on simplifying an overly complicated human reality. In fact, a phenomenon that cannot be simplified in order to generalise, cannot typically be modelled effectively as an AI algorithm.

All models are wrong – since generalisation always leaves room for mistakes, and leave out outliers. Even a highly accurate AI algorithm, yielding an accuracy level of 95% for example, is still expected to be wrong 5% of the time. If its accuracy level is higher than that, it might very well be due to what we call 'over-fitting', which means that the model is very tied to the nature of the specific dataset it was trained on. This will make it very hard to generalise to slightly different datasets.

Generalisation might be useful to solve some problems, but it might also easily become an over-generalisation. At this point, we would argue that, more probably – **all models are wrong, some are useful, and many of them are dangerous**.

Simplifying and generalising human phenomena are the strongest weapons of machine learning. At the same time, they might also be totally missing the point. Let's have a look at two examples of how modelling and generalisation can make AI models dangerous. We name the first 'reducing the irreducible' and the second 'stop the world – I want to get off'.

REDUCING THE IRREDUCIBLE

One way in which human intelligence is superior to machine's intelligence is in our ability to grasp the essence of hugely complicated human phenomena. More accurately, humans have a much stronger ability to do so without the necessity to break it down into observable components, so they can see the forest, despite the trees.

Humans are able to think abstractly and to develop intuitions based on their experience, their learned <u>heuristics</u> and their affective reactions to complex phenomena such as human behaviours. Interestingly enough, we sometimes do it without even being able to identify what were the exact observations or pieces of evidence that led us to reach a specific conclusion. An example of such a human phenomenon could be teachers judging students' engagement. When asked, a teacher could form an informed opinion on their student's engagement. They would be able to tell you which student is more or less engaged with several types of subjects or activities but might struggle to put their finger on a specific set of observations that informed their opinion.

On the other hand, an <u>AIED system</u> trying to establish an informed 'opinion' about students' engagement, does not have any 'experience', 'emotion' or 'intuition'. Instead, the AI developer will try to pin down which indicators or observations could be used by the system to measure engagement. Obviously, this is a challenging task. First, just defining what 'student engagement' means is a difficult task by itself and one which many learning sciences researchers are still struggling to agree on. Second, as for many social constructs, student engagement is an extremely complex construct, and most probably is composed of several components (such as student's engagement with the learning material, with their teachers, with their peers, with their surrounding world) and dimensions (such as student's participation in class, active listening, engaging in discussions in class or online, independently researching and more). Third, measuring mental processes (such as listening and researching) is mostly not possible, for technical and ethical reasons. For these reasons, AI developers will need to reduce a highly complicated, multi-dimensional mental human construct (such as students' engagement) to a set of externally visible and measurable metrics known as proxies.

In our student's engagement example, the developer will need to understand what data points they can use to feed the AI algorithm. As an example, one set of proxies could be composed of the frequency a student participated in a class discussion, a student's eye movements while in class, and the number of times a student approached their teacher to ask for some clarification or feedback.

Obviously, there is no way to model such complex phenomena without measurable (or quantifiable) ways to measure merely an approximate version of our human behaviours and traits. On the other hand, some human phenomena could not (or should not) be reduced to a narrow set of measures. Omitting some important aspects of students' engagement just because they are hard to measure (such as listening) and assigning so-called 'objective' numbers to culturally dependent constructs such as engagement might yield irrelevant, or worse – very wrong results. Going back to our model of students' engagement, its chosen measures (such as frequency of help-seeking, or eye-gaze patterns) might be strongly affected by culture, time zones, Internet availability, language, personality, learning difficulty and so many more factors that might bias the AI's ability to grasp engagement.

These factors, when not being accounted for in a model, go unnoticed not just by those designing the AI system but also by those using it. Therefore, not only does reducing the irreducible impose a very tangible danger to using AI systems [4], but it also raises a very legitimate question about whether AI should be used at all in such cases.

As a note to AI system designers and developers – if you find a social or educational construct easy to measure, you are probably not capturing its full essence.

STOP THE WORLD – I WANT TO GET OFF!

Most often, human behaviours are not only complicated but also unpredictable. Most human behaviours change, evolve and regress. Most human behaviours (such as engagement in our example) are actually a set of intertwined processes, rather than something that can be captured in a single snapshot in time. In other words, modelling social or educational constructs not only rely on simplification and generalisation but also on the ability to understand dynamic systems by looking at them statically.

For example, when training a supervised machine-learning model, the model trains on a specific dataset. What happens to the model when the dataset changes? Moreover, what happens when the assumptions about what consists of a 'normal' baseline to this behaviour changes?

The COVID-19 pandemic is an excellent example of the shortcomings of modelling human behaviour that might change. After COVID hit, the norms for students' engagement were utterly challenged. The teaching and learning reality changed so dramatically due to remote learning settings, teachers' training gaps, students' varied opportunities to access the Internet, and their ability to study from home [5]. Engagement now looked completely different, measuring it would have been completely different, and the established norms and baselines changed forever. How often do we come across an AI system (for example – which is based on students' engagement modelling) that was adopted due to the new evidence and assumptions about engagement post-COVID? Not often. Moreover, when students and teachers came back to their classes, they were different. They had now learned about how they feel or think about engaging differently. Educational systems and educational technology did not learn as fast. Is it schools' job to de-teach them in order for them to go back and engage based on their previous assumptions just so that the status quo could remain intact?

AI systems are not just designed to simplify and generalise, but also to impose order, 'logical sense', certainty and stability to a highly messy, ambiguous and unpredictable human reality [4]. This is not surprising, since it is in a certain and simple world where AI excels. However, it is our (human) responsibility to make sure we are not forcing a dynamic reality into a static modelling straitjacket.

Also, however much we, the authors, might wish it, it is not always in others' interest to bring the whole dynamics and complexity of human behaviour into AI systems. Some vested interests or political groups might prefer a more static image of humanity. Breaking glass ceilings and mobilising between social classes is not always considered desirable, and the EdTech market is not unaffected by this view.

THE EDUCATIONAL TOWER OF BABEL

In Chapter 1, we discussed the affordances of educational technologies. We discussed how the affordances of traditional educational technologies are relatively straightforward: a pencil is for writing in a notebook and a piece of chalk and a blackboard are for writing in front of a classroom. We also discussed how the world of learning affordances becomes more complicated when modern educational technologies, such as AI, enter the classroom. Now different users will be afforded different possibilities from the same AI system, which makes evaluating it more complex.

A similar argument holds for the complexity of the whole educational ecosystem. "*It takes a village to raise a child*" is a traditional saying, reflecting the number and variety of people that should be involved in raising a single child. In an educational world not dominated by technology, it is well known that carers, teachers, healthcare practitioners – all need to be engaged in a meaningful dialogue around learners.

In an EdTech-dominated world, however, this dialog cannot remain relevant without engaging technology developers and designers. The 'village' is now a highly complex network of carers, educators and other professionals, but also full of devices collecting data about the learners and technologies designed to assist them. The 'village' of teachers and carers cannot afford anymore to stay away from assuming a secondary role of facilitating the use of those technologies, in order to maintain a meaningful dialogue around learners.

Once AI comes into the picture, there is yet another 'type of intelligence' flowing in this new network of people and technologies. There is a need now to embrace a new level of complexity and learn a whole new language.

Translating the languages of students, teachers, carers and other professionals is no longer enough. People 'growing up' in the technology sector have been acquiring their own language. AI has its own language. In order to maintain this meaningful dialogue around learners, an overly complicated educational tower of Babel needs to be built and nurtured carefully, and a new shared language needs to be carefully formed. This is exactly what we have tried to do in this book: to bring together different languages into having a shared meaningful dialogue around learners.

If this book has opened more questions than it has given answers, it means for us that the goal has been reached and a new dialogue has begun.

The new 'AI' elephant toy that has tried to find its place and role between Bella, Mrs Tunningham and the good old cuddly elephant – finally got to have a place within this new dialogue. A place still full of suspicions and potential, but a secure place around the table.

Throughout Chapters 2, 3 and 4, we have questioned the place of the AI elephant within the educational dialogue around learners. We asked whether it could take the role of a learner, the role of a tutor and can it assume the role of a classroom moderator. No doubt, if the book had been longer, we could (and should) ask whether it can take the role of a classmate, a role of a smart textbook, a role of a smart classroom, a role of an exams' assessor and many other teaching and administrative roles within the educational ecosystem.

In any of those roles, there could not have been a meaningful discussion without including all of the educational stakeholders: the learners, their carers, their teachers, educational leaders, systems designers and developers. The new complex ecosystem must be maintained with all of its inherent complexity.

But the tower of Babel must have a sustainable and strong infrastructure. Bridging between various disciplines and professions requires trust. To establish this trust, we have outlined the use of an analytical, evidence-based approach to evaluating AI systems within the classroom and to making an informed choice of how to design such systems, and how to integrate them within the desired pedagogies. Our five-step process (appearing here again, after being introduced in Chapter 1, and applied in Chapters 2 to 4) is our attempt to

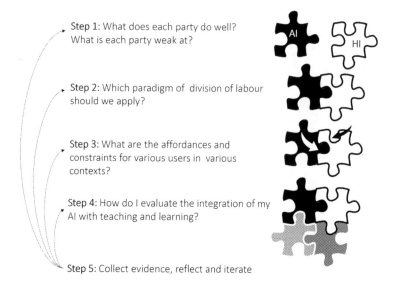

Step 1: What does each party do well? What is each party weak at?

Step 2: Which paradigm of division of labour should we apply?

Step 3: What are the affordances and constraints for various users in various contexts?

Step 4: How do I evaluate the integration of my AI with teaching and learning?

Step 5: Collect evidence, reflect and iterate

Figure 5.2 Five iterative steps in assessing AI in learning and teaching.

suggest an instrumental, pragmatic approach to making sure that the human intelligence is the one who designs, orchestrates, and evaluates machine's intelligence, and not the other way around (Figure 5.2).

POSTSCRIPT

This has been a short book and we have had to be very selective about which aspects of AI in education that we described. Three areas that did not receive much attention were (i) the applications of AI that help educational administrators do their job, (ii) the use of AI as a laboratory to help teachers and to develop educational theory and (iii) AI as an examiner.

ADMINISTRATOR-FACING SYSTEMS

Chapters 2, 3 and 4 gave plenty of examples of learner-facing systems such as learners and tutors, and teacher-facing systems such as orchestration tools. There is a third group within education who also can be helped by AI and these are educational administrators and managers. They use systems to understand the data from whole cohorts of learners as opposed to orchestration systems that work with individual classes. For example, such systems can use the pattern-finding capabilities of AI applied to very large numbers of students. One example is to identify trends in student behaviour that are early indicators of failure or dropout so that potential difficulties can be headed off in a timely fashion. As with all such diagnostic systems there will be both false positives and false negatives. It is important that there is a human in the loop to decide whether the diagnosis of failure or dropout looks plausible, given the other contextual information that is available. A human is also needed to find out, from the student, why his or her pattern of behaviour changed and whether there is some other explanation than discontent or lack of motivation that might warrant a different supportive approach.

AI AS A LABORATORY

In Chapter 2, we mentioned that trainee teachers can practice their craft by teaching simulated learners, monitoring the results and then adjusting their approach as necessary. AI can be used as a laboratory in a wider sense too. Many of the teaching strategies and tactics that have been used in AI-based tutors and teachers have been derived from observations of expert human tutors and teachers. These have been codified to a sufficient degree of detail that they can then be programmed into such systems. Given the possibility that many students might use such systems, experiments can be run to test out different tactics and strategies to see which work best, in a way that would be much harder to do through using human teachers and tutors.

Of course, there is a big social and psychological difference between being taught by a human and being taught by a system, potentially pretending to act like a human. Both praise and blame from a human teacher just feel different than when the same words are uttered by an online pedagogical agent. In our own work, we found that some tactics which could usefully be used by a human teacher were not responded too well when tried by an AI-based teacher. Notable among these was the leaner's much more negative reaction to a system's refusal to help compared to a human teacher's refusal to help when the system or the human thought that the learner did not need help.

AI AS AN EXAMINER

The recent 'exams fiasco' in England has demonstrated some of the issues around using AI as part of the examination process. Because national exams had been cancelled due to COVID, it was felt that there needed to be some reliable substitute method for allocating grades. This was of particular concern for students who had applied to university and who needed to achieve particular grade outcomes to match their conditional offers. The fact that the English school and higher-education system is so focused on examinations and grading is a much bigger issue than can be explored here. The initial idea was that teachers would use their best skill and judgement as well as any existing results, such as from mock exams, to allocate grades for the exams that the students were not able to sit. Then there was a worry that some teachers might inflate the grades of their students, based on the idea that teachers, as humans, have their biases and indeed may be pressured to do so.

To counteract this problem, a system was developed to analyse previous results for each school and subject cohort and overlay this on to the teachers' predicted grades. So for example, if a particular school had always done rather well in teaching history in the past, then high teacher predicted grades for history were regarded as plausible. In a similar fashion, if a school had historically done rather badly in geography then high teacher predicted grades were regarded as implausible.

The 'mutant algorithm' did what it said on the tin, and its predictions overall were perfectly reasonable. The injustice of this bore down particularly on bright and committed students attending a school with a historically poor track record; their high predicted grades looked implausible and some students were marked down severely. There was a different injustice for not-so-bright students in schools with good track records, as their teacher predicted poor grades also looked implausible but they were the marked up. There was a lot of upset and eventually it was decided to abandon the use of the algorithm, though not before some of the injustices had fed through to some students being denied conditional places at university.

The moral here is that the algorithm worked well in predicting general trends (hence, it was 'accurate'), but the trends were designed to generalize and smooth away outliers, such as good students in poor schools. By that, it perpetuated an existing status quo and prevented new opportunities for social mobility. In the end, the fairest way was adopted where humans in the loop (teachers) made the predictions even though there was a general trend towards grade inflation.

REFERENCES

1. Clark, M. (2021, April 8). Students of color are getting flagged to their teachers because testing software can't see them. THE VERGE. https://www.theverge.com/2021/4/8/22374386/proctorio-racial-bias-issues-open cv-facial-detection-schools-tests-remote-learning; https://www.blumen thal.senate.gov/imo/media/doc/2020.12.3%20Letter%20to%20Ed %20Testing%20Software%20Companies%20ExamSoft.pdf

2. Wikipedia. 2020 UK GCSE and A-Level grading controversy. https://en. wikipedia.org/wiki/2020_UK_GCSE_and_A-Level_grading_controversy

3. Karumbaiah, S., & Brooks, J. (2021). How colonial continuities under-lie Algorithmic injustices in education. In RESPECT 2021. Retrieved from http://respect2021.stcbp.org/wp-content/uploads/2021/05/201_Posi-tion_Papers_01_paper_73.pdf

4. Birhane, A. (2021). The impossibility of Automating Ambiguity. *Artificial Life*, 27(1), 44–61.

5. Kent, C., Luckin, R., Blake, C., George, K., Lepkowska, D., Anthony, S., Fisher, A. & Wells, R. (2021). Shock to the System: Lessons from Covid-19. EDUCATE Ventures Research and Cambridge Partnership for Education. https://www.educateventures.com/lessons-from-covid-19

GLOSSARY

AI expert system: an expert system stems from the concept of a machine or an algorithm mimicking human intelligence. Usually, it would be mimicking a certain part in the process of the decision-making (such as reasoning or inferring) of a human expert, whose expertise is in (typically) one knowledge domain (such as education and medicine). Expert systems became quite popular during the eighties and the nineties of the 20th century and were mostly built on top of a set of human-curated logical rules (see **rule-based systems**).

AIED (AI in Education) conceptual architecture: refers to a simplified architecture of an AIED system. It consists of a pedagogical model, a domain model, a learner model, together with an interface through which the system and the learner or learners communicate. The pedagogical model expresses teaching methods, the domain model expresses the taught subject knowledge and the learner model embodies the changing cognitive, affective and behavioural attributes of the learner.

Algorithm: a sequence of rules and calculations carried out by a computer program in order to solve a problem or carry out an automatic task.

Artificial intelligence (AI): refers to pieces of software or hardware (such as computer programs or robots) that might appear as if they are acting or thinking humanly.

Authoring system: is a software system for building an educational application (for example it might include an interface for an expert to author their own set of logical rules, which they wish to enrich an AI system with).

Autonomy: the power to decide, striking a balance between the decision-making power we retain for ourselves and that which we delegate to artificial agents.

Beneficence: doing good: promoting well-being, preserving dignity and sustaining the planet.

Classroom orchestration: refers to the management of classroom workflows, involving small group, individual and whole-class activities.

Concept map: is a diagrammatic way of setting out how concepts are related to each other.

The data-driven approach to AI (inductive reasoning): pertains to a machine collecting sample of data points or observations, and inferring some general logic out of them.

Domain knowledge: is what an AIED system knows about the subject or topic to be taught.

Explicability: enabling a safe AI system through intelligibility, transparency and accountability.

Heuristics: are simplified rules to help get things done. They may not always work, but they are simple to apply.

Human–AI transactive collaboration HI–AI collaboration paradigm: a well-defined division of labour, based on a differential analysis of both AI and humans' skill sets.

The human-in-the-loop HI–AI collaboration paradigm: The focus is on when and to what extent humans take part in the AI pipeline.

The hybrid intelligence HI–AI collaboration paradigm: the synergetic combination of human and artificial agents, being strongly intertwined.

If–Then–Else rules: are logical rules, designed to be consumed easily by algorithms. If–Then–Else rules usually adhere to the basic casual structure of 'IF (condition) THEN (conclusion).' For example: IF (score in question 1 > 10) THEN (sufficient level of knowledge is in place). However, when used in rule-based AI systems, they could become very complex, ambiguous, and even conflicting. Therefore, although If–Then–Else rules are designed to be understandable by humans, and crafted from human logic, they may become difficult to read and comprehend by humans.

The intelligent prosthetics/extension HI–AI collaboration paradigm: aims at allowing humans to 'scale up' and act more effectively (e.g. in tasks such as decision-support, automation or quicken originally human-based processes).

The Interface (in an AIED system): the means through which the learner and the system can communicate.

Justice: preserving solidarity, avoiding unfairness, relating to the use of AI to correct past wrongs such as eliminating unfair discrimination, promoting diversity and preventing the rise of new threats to justice.

A Label: is one special piece of information associated with each record in a dataset. It is special for serving as an indication, usually created by a human expert, to 'teach' a supervised ML algorithm how we – humans – would typically classify or relate to this record. For example, if our aim is to train an ML algorithm to identify the presence of cats in images, we would start by feeding it with a dataset of images, to train on – some including cats and some not. In order to 'teach' the algorithm how to identify images with cats, a human being would label this initial training dataset, by indicating whether each image contains a cat or not. The ML algorithm would in turn 'train' on this humanly labelled dataset. As a result of this training, when shown a new (unlabelled) image (which is merely a random set of pixels for the algorithm), the ML will try to make 'an educated guess' on whether it includes a cat or not, all following the logic it learned by observing the labelled images it processed beforehand.

Learner model, student model: is that component of an AIED system that captures what it knows about the learner.

Learning affordance: is a learning-related ability a user perceives to be achievable as a result of interacting with a particular technology.

Learning sciences: is an academic discipline focused on the processes around effective or ineffective human learning, and its implications on the design and implementation of learning tools and instructional methodologies.

The logic-drive approach to AI (deductive reasoning): is the foundation of the traditional 'top-down logic', which consists of the application of general logic to observations.

Machine learning (ML): is a subfield of artificial intelligence. It is the most widely used artificial intelligence method in the last 20 years, and it is based mostly on data-driven reasoning, in that ML models are developed on the basis of statistical patterns observed in datasets.

Metacognition, metacognitive capability: is the learner's capability to think about what they know and to manage or regulate the way they go about learning.

Multimodal: originated from multiple data sources and types (for example, from a tutoring system, a learning management system and video).

Non-maleficence: (not doing harm): privacy, security and 'capability caution', cautions against various negative consequences of overusing or misusing AI technologies.

Orchestrated systems: are systems that could be orchestrated by an <u>orchestrating system</u>. For example, a tutoring system might be orchestrated by sending data about students' progress to an orchestrating system that would use it to help teachers manage their classroom.

Orchestrating systems: work to support teachers in managing the classroom. This could be done by monitoring the flow of the lesson, alerting on important events taking place in class that the teacher would struggle to spot, or showing the teacher fine-grained information on the progress each student is making in more than one system.

Pedagogical model: is that component of an AIED system that contains the rules about how to teach and help the learner.

A rule-based AI architecture: was one of the most widely used AI systems before machine learning became popular. It typically employs the logic-based approach. An algorithm is fed a set of rules encompassing knowledge about a specific domain (usually generated by experts). The algorithm then applies those rules to new observations and typically results in recommendations or insights. Most rules would be structured as an If–Then–Else rules. One of the first-known AI rule-based systems was MYCIN, which was a medical diagnostic expert system. MYCIN was based on several hundred rules, curated from discussions with human medical experts.

The SAMR framework: was devised by Dr Puentedura, who distinguished four levels of classroom technology integration: Substitution, Augmentation, Modification and Redefinition.

Schema is a type of a hueristic and: is a mental representation of concepts that humans use to store in their long-term memory, so they can quickly extract them and use them during the course of their daily lives. Children with exposure to books for most of their lives will develop a schema in their minds of what a book is. In this book schema, pages are gathered together, each with some text or images, generally encoding stories or other types of information. When getting a new book, a child who has already acquired the schema of a book would unconsciously extract it from their long-term memory, and would therefore know what to do with it. However, when a child meets an e-book for the first time, they would probably need to adjust their existing book schema to grasp the digital format and to adapt to a new set of affordances and limitations.

Script: is a type of schema for events. In other words, a script is a sequence of behaviours, we – human beings – mentally attach to a given situation. In this sense, it is another mental short-cut (heuristics) that allows us to deal with everyday events without having to learn what to do every day from scratch. As an example, a child who has been going to school for some time knows what is the script for arriving at school. They know that when they arrive in the morning, they are expected to go into the classroom, sit near their desk, and wait for an adult to come and guide them. If they haven't stored this script in their long-term memory, they would be extremely anxious to go to school every morning, without having any certainty or expectation about what is going to happen.

Self-regulated learning: refers to the capability of being able to understand, regulate and potentially transfer one's learning.

Supervised machine learning: refers to the process by which the ML algorithm is trained on a dataset that was labelled in advance usually by a human expert.

Technological affordance: in our context refers to the perceived and actual properties of a technology, which determine just how it could be used.

Technology Affordances and Constraints Theory (TACT): has shed some light on the significance of limitations imposed on technologies in addition to their affordances.

Thinking machines HI–AI collaboration paradigm: achieve human goals like humans do (e.g. expert systems, conversational bots, IBM Jeopardy, IBM Debater, IBM Deep Blue, Alpha Go).

TPACK (Technological, Pedagogical and Content Knowledge: by Mishra and Koehler) is designed to identify a technology-based instructional strategy, based on the view of teaching as an interactional model between what teachers know, how they apply what they know and the unique context of their classroom.

TPCA(D)K (Technological, Pedagogical, Content and Data Knowledge): represents an emergent form of the TPACK model that combines a fourth component, the Data Knowledge.

Training: (an ML algorithm) is the process by which the algorithm processes a set of data records and identifies statistical patterns hidden in them. A set of such statistical patterns might be called an ML Model.

Tutoring systems: are AIED systems that act as either teachers or tutors. They also have the more specialised meaning of embodying a particular style of teaching problem-solving in which mistakes are commented on immediately.

Unsupervised machine learning: refers to the process by which the ML algorithm is trained on a dataset that was not labelled in advance. Unlike supervised ML, the process of 'learning' the patterns in the data is not supervised by any 'prescriptive' human logic.

INDEX